WALKING IN THE AOSTA VALLEY

WALKS AND SCRAMBLES IN THE SHADOWS OF
MONT BLANC, THE MATTERHORN AND
MONTE ROSA

WALKING IN THE AOSTA VALLEY

WALKS AND SCRAMBLES IN THE SHADOWS OF MONT BLANC, THE MATTERHORN AND MONTE ROSA

by Andy Hodges

JUNIPER HOUSE, MURLEY MOSS,
OXENHOLME ROAD, KENDAL, CUMBRIA LA9 7RL
www.cicerone.co.uk

© Andy Hodges 2022
First edition 2022
ISBN: 978 1 78631 015 6

Printed in Singapore by KHL Printing on responsibly sourced paper
A catalogue record for this book is available from the British Library.
All photographs are by the author unless otherwise stated.
Author photo credit: Anne Hughes

Route mapping by Lovell Johns www.lovelljohns.com
Contains OpenStreetMap.org data © OpenStreetMap
contributors, CC-BY-SA. NASA relief data courtesy of ESRI

Updates to this Guide

While every effort is made by our authors to ensure the accuracy of guidebooks as they go to print, changes can occur during the lifetime of an edition. This guidebook was in part researched and written before the COVID-19 pandemic. While we are not aware of any significant changes to routes or facilities at the time of printing, it is likely that the current situation will give rise to more changes than would usually be expected. Any updates that we know of for this guide will be on the Cicerone website (www.cicerone.co.uk/1015/updates), so please check before planning your trip. We also advise that you check information about such things as transport, accommodation and shops locally. Even rights of way can be altered over time.

We are always grateful for information about any discrepancies between a guidebook and the facts on the ground, sent by email to updates@cicerone.co.uk or by post to Cicerone, Juniper House, Murley Moss, Oxenholme Road, Kendal, LA9 7RL.

Register your book: to sign up to receive free updates, special offers and GPX files where available, register your book at www.cicerone.co.uk. The route maps in this guide are derived from publicly available data, databases and crowd-sourced data. As such they have not been through the detailed checking procedures that would generally be applied to a published map from an official mapping agency. However, we have reviewed them closely in the light of local knowledge as part of the preparation of this guide.

Front cover: Mont Blanc from Mont de la Saxe

CONTENTS

Mountain safety

Every mountain walk has its dangers, and those described in this guidebook are no exception. All who walk or climb in the mountains should recognise this and take responsibility for themselves and their companions along the way. The author and publisher have made every effort to ensure that the information contained in this guide was correct when it went to press, but, except for any liability that cannot be excluded by law, they cannot accept responsibility for any loss, injury or inconvenience sustained by any person using this book.

International distress signal *(emergency only)*
Six blasts on a whistle (and flashes with a torch after dark) spaced evenly for one minute, followed by a minute's pause. Repeat until an answer is received. The response is three signals per minute followed by a minute's pause.

Helicopter rescue
The following signals are used to communicate with a helicopter:

Help needed:
raise both arms
above head to
form a 'Y'

Help not needed:
raise one arm
above head, extend
other arm downward

Emergency telephone numbers
If telephoning from the UK the dialling codes are:
Italy: 0039; *France:* 0033; *Switzerland:* 0041

Italy: Carabinieri: tel 0165 84 22 25; Emergency Services: tel 118
France: PGHM (Peloton de Gendarmerie de Haute Montagne):
tel 04 50 53 16 89; Emergency services: tel 112 (mobile phones)
Switzerland: OCVS (Organisation Cantonale Valaisanne de Secours): tel 144

Weather reports
Italy: tel 0165 44 113
France: Chamonix: tel 08 92 68 02 74, www.meteo.fr or tel 3250
Switzerland: tel 162 (in French, German or Italian), www.meteoschweiz.ch/en

Mountain rescue can be very expensive – be adequately insured.

Dedication

Thank you to my Lucas family (Aunty Joan and Uncle John, Aunty Barb and Uncle Paul and Uncle Ted) for buying me my first climbing rope at eighteen. Without it I might never have begun to explore the mountains, so it was probably the best present ever!

Also, thank you to my adopted Aunty and Uncle, Linda and Michael Ladyman for my first guidebook to walking in the Lake District – every serious walker needs Wainwright's words of wisdom. I hope the words in this book help folk discover another beautiful mountain area.

The final ridge section to Mont Mars (Route 6)

ROUTE SUMMARY TABLE

Walk no	Route	Start/Finish	Grade	Time	Distance	Height gain	Height loss	Page
Main Valley								
1	Forte di Bard and the Roman road	Donnas	1	1hr 20min	4.5km	30m	30m	46
2	Napoleon's diversion route	Bard	2	3hr 45min	9km	640m	640m	51
Lower Lys Valley								
3	Plan des Sorcières and Col Portola	Etoile du Berger, Sassa	1+	2hr 40min – 3hr 40min	9km	610m	610m	57
4	The Two Monts: Mont Roux and Mont Bechit	Etoile du Berger, Sassa	2	5hr 15min	10km	1030m	1030m	61
5	Colma di Monbarone	Etoile du Berger, Sassa	2+	5hr 45min	11.5km	965m	965m	66
6	Mont Mars traverse	Coumarial	3	Day 1: 2hr 45min Day 2: 6hr 35min	5km7km	1400m	1400m	71
Upper Lys Valley								
7	Via Regina to Castel Savoia	Gressoney-Saint-Jean	1	1hr 20min	3.5km	40m	40m	81
8	Punta Regina: the queen's peak	Weissmatten chairlift	2	3hr 20min	6km	505m	505m	84
9	Alpenzu and the Walser villages	Gressoney-Saint-Jean	2	4hr 10min	12.5km	540m	540m	90
10	Source of the Lys	Staffal	2	3hr	6km	600m	600m	96
11	Punta Indren and the Indren glacier crossing	Staffal:S: Passo dei Salati lift stationF: Indren lift station	3 F	1hr 45min plus lifts: 2hr 45min	2.5km	420m	70m	100

Walk no	Route	Start/Finish	Grade	Time	Distance	Height gain	Height loss	Page
12	Bettolina Ridge to Rifugio Quintino Sella	Passo di Bettaforca, lift station	3 F	5hr 30min	8km	980m	980m	105
Valtournenche								
13	Eastern balcony: Cervinia to Valtournenche	S:Breuil-CerviniaF: Valtournenche	2	5hr 15min	13km	350m	840m	113
14	Western balcony: Cervinia to Valtournenche	S:Breuil-CerviniaF: Valtournenche	2	5hr 15min	14km	570m	1100m	118
15	Becca d'Aran	Cheneil car parking	2 (3 to summit)	4hr 55min	9km	970m	970m	122
Valpelline								
16	Rifugio Prarayer	Place Moulin Dam	1	2hr 20min or (3hr 20min incl extension)	9km or (12.5km incl ext)	160m or (230m incl ext)	160m or (230m incl ext)	127
17	Ru di-z-Aagne and Fontina	S: Chozod-SemonF: Ollomont	1	1hr 45min	5 km	300m	30m	131
18	Lac Mort	Place Moulin Dam	2	3hr 45min	7.5km	1050m	1050m	134
19	Ru du Rey: a marvel of hydro-engineering	Rey/Ollomont	2	4hr 40min	14 km	710m	710m	138
20	Pointe Cornet	Rey/Ollomont	2	4hr 50min	13 km	1050m	1050m	143
21	Alta Via 1: Col de Breuson	S: Les Sergnoux (Closé)F: Ollomont	2	5hr 15min	11km	1080m	1150m	149
22	Rifugio and Col Champillon	Plan Détruit	1 (2 to col)	1hr 35min (3hr incl col)	4.5km (6.5km incl col)	360m (635mincl col)	360m (635mincl col)	154

Walk no	Route	Start/Finish	Grade	Time	Distance	Height gain	Height loss	Page
Great St Bernard Pass								
23	Via Francigena to Great St Bernard Monastery	S: Saint-OyenF: Great St Bernard Monastery	2	4hr 30min	11km	1160m	30m	160
24	Mont Fourchon	Roadside car park, Baou	2+	3hr 15min	4km	550m	550m	167
25	Two Cols	Car park on roadside near La Cantina	23 nav	4hr 10min	9km	620m	620m	170
26	Grande Chenalette and Pointe de Drône via ferrata	Great St Bernard Monastery	F(PD continuation)	4hr 55min	6km	600m	600m	176
Courmayeur								
27	Mont Chétif	Courmayeur	2+	5hr 10min	10.5km	1200m	1200m	182
28	Mont de la Saxe and Col Sapin	Courmayeur	2	6hr 30min	12km	1100m	1100m	186
29	Rifugio Bonatti and Mont Blanc panorama	Lavachey car park/bus stop	2	2hr 35min to4hr 55min	6 km/11 km	390m/540m	390m/950m	190
30	Mont Fortin	Chalet del Miage	3	6hr 25min	19.5km	1250m	1250m	197
31	Tour of the Pyramides Calcaires	Chalet del Miage	2	5hr 30min	19km	950m	950m	203
32	Mont Chétif via ferrata	Courmayeur	F	6hr 25min	6km	1200m	600m	208

11

Mont Blanc makes an appearance through the trees (Routes 27 and 32)

INTRODUCTION

Mont Blanc towering over Mont Chétif from Col Sapin (Route 28)

With its head firmly set among the clouds of Monte Bianco and the Italian plains spreading from the valley mouth, the Aosta valley has been a determined travellers' thoroughfare for millennia. Some say Hannibal used the valley as his gateway to Rome (although this has largely been debunked today). The Roman Empire certainly understood the importance of the valley and its pathway to Gaul; the imposing town of Aosta was built to guard the pass and enforce the Pax Romana. It was very much an Alpine capital and, to some extent, continues to be one today. Pilgrims from Canterbury were regular visitors on their way to Rome, thankful for the safe crossing of the notorious Great St Bernard Pass or, on the return route, more than ready and willing to pray, and pay, for a safe return over the col. The Great St Bernard Hospice (or monastery), located at the pass, became renowned for saving unfortunate travellers with the help of the specially bred (and now world-famous) St Bernard dog. As a result, both the monastery and dog breed are celebrated throughout history.

With a backdrop of pure white peaks, each of the valleys that forms the saw-toothed ridge separating Italy and Switzerland is waiting to welcome you. While the highest peaks may be beyond the regular hillwalker, the region welcomes walkers of all standards and plenty of summits are within the abilities of regular walkers, each walk offering views to last a lifetime.

As well as offering typical Italian hospitality, the region has a unique Savoyard flavour. Until a little over 150 years ago the valley was a key part of the House of Savoy and lasting reflections of this are abundant to this day. Not least is the bilingual nature of the area: French will serve the intrepid independent traveller well although an attempt at Italian will be warmly welcomed.

Extensive Roman remains make Aosta an interesting town to explore; the medieval towers and streets are a delight to discover while the centre hosts an impressive range of shops and attractions. Of particular interest to the mountain adventurer will be the outlet shops of several Italian equipment manufacturers.

GEOGRAPHY

The Aosta valley is much longer than might be expected. From the Piedmont plain it stretches over 90km and gains over 1000m in altitude passing through Courmayeur to reach the foot of Mont Blanc. The Dora Baltea river rises from the foot of Mont Blanc and flows for 170km to join the River Po.

The numerous valleys that join from the north are longer than any found in British mountains. The valley

Looking down the valley from Rifugio Prarayer (Route 16)

The Matterhorn from the summit of Becca d'Aran (Route 15)

leading to the Great St Bernard Pass (Colle del Gran San Bernardo) is one of the longest at 34km in length. In days gone by this would have taken at least three days to cross; today it is little more than an hour and a half in a car. These valleys are home to many beautiful villages nestled into the hillsides and are the base for a multitude of walks: from short hour-long ambles to routes reaching the foot of mighty glaciers tumbling from the highest peaks.

To the south of the main valley lies the beautiful Gran Paradiso National Park, covered by Gillian Price's equally inspiring Cicerone guidebook, *Walking and Trekking in Gran Paradiso*.

The northern Aosta valleys
The significant valleys to the north of the main valley are, from east to west:

The Lys valley
Gressoney-Saint-Jean in the upper valley is the main village. There is host of walking and alpinism routes in the valley while the ski lift system at Staffal allows access to the snowline even in high summer.

The Ayas valley
Champoluc is a ski resort where many skiers begin their skiing careers. It remains a popular resort and the ski infrastructure allows easy access to the high mountains in the summer but

detracts from the mountain environment to some extent.

Valtournenche

Breuil-Cervinia lies at the head of the valley and is a well-known ski centre. Cervin (the Matterhorn) sits above the town and is often shrouded by mist in the afternoons. With summer skiing on offer, as well as mountain-bike trails leading from the ski stations, there is plenty to keep the more active busy, while quiet tracks and trails can be enjoyed in seclusion and tranquillity.

Valpelline

Although a less well-known valley, it has a surprising amount of walking on offer. Quiet, majestic and scenic, this valley is a secret waiting to be discovered. A very pleasant campsite makes a cost-effective base with plenty of walks and stunning views on the doorstep.

Great St Bernard Pass

One of the most famous valleys in the Alps, if not the world, it has been a major thoroughfare for thousands of years and echoes to the footsteps of pilgrims passing along the Via Francigena to this day. Walkers can experience an unforgettable night staying in, and exploring, the most iconic of mountain monasteries.

Val Ferret/Val Veny

This is the final valley within the northern side of the Valle d'Aosta. On

Stained-glass art installation on the Via Francigena, Saint-Rhémy-en-Bosses (Route 23)

a clear day the view of the peaks of the Mont Blanc range is a veritable who's who of mountain first ascents.

GEOLOGY

The complex geology of the Alps is a book in itself; a geologically young range of mountains, which are still growing, they offer a fascinating insight into the power of nature.

Crystal hunting was one of the reasons for ascending the high mountains in the past, which gave birth to mountaineering. Geologists believe significant gold fields exist under Monte Rosa, and an abandoned gold mine can be found near the Etoile du Berger in the lower Lys valley.

Col Champillon and Mont Blanc in the distance (Route 22)

The Alps began to form into a mountain range when the Tethys Sea existed between what is now Africa and Europe. This warm, shallow sea was the perfect environment for the development of deep layers of limestone. The sea began to reduce as the African tectonic plate moved north during the Palaeogene period. Over the course of around 35 million years, the sea's sediments evolved into layered sedimentary rocks; these folded over on each other, creating nappes (layers of rock that have completely folded over rock that was originally above it), causing geologically confusing profiles, where younger rock ends up beneath older rock. These rocks were later subjected to intense heat and pressure forming various metamorphic rocks, including gneiss and schist.

The resultant layering of rock means that the summit rocks of the Matterhorn were originally part of the African Plate, while those lower on the mountain originate from the ancient seabed of the Tethys Sea, with rock from the Eurasian Plate forming the midlayer.

The gradual growth in height of the mountains eventually resulted in a significant mountain range. It is estimated that this growth is continuing at a rate of about 2mm per year.

Glaciation has continued to erode the mountains; it is hard to imagine even the highest peaks being submerged by immense glaciers reaching as far as Lyon in France. Following the end of the last ice age the mountains began to form into the range we see today. Glacial retreat caused enormous amounts of rockfall, and the peaks 'sharpened' into the present shape. Humans then began to move into the valleys and settle.

In recent times glacial retreat and advance has caused changes at a human level. Up until the 1200–1300s the high passes were crossable in summer; however, during the last mini ice age the passes became blocked by ice and snow, and people in the Walser region were unable to return to the Upper Valais. The passes remain icebound today and the Walser valleys maintain a unique character owing much to their Germanic/Swiss origins; this is particularly apparent in the Lys valley.

Both Monte Rosa and Mont Blanc owe their colouring and immense bulk to their geology. Formed from ultra-tough granite, they resisted glacial erosion and as such are the two highest mountain massifs in the Alps.

WILDLIFE

One of the joys of travelling in the mountains is the occasional unexpected encounter with the local wildlife.

The iconic marmot will delight the traveller with its antics and panic-stricken whistles at every perceived threat. This subterranean,

Alpine marmot in its natural environment, rocky terrain above 1800m

colony-living member of the rodent family is comical in its manner. Its shrill whistle will probably be the first encounter for most walkers. A sentry can often be seen on a high outcrop or grassy knoll while members of the colony feed on the vegetation. When a predator or other threat is perceived, the whistle will send the grazers scuttling for the cover of their burrows.

The majestic ibex may be seen surveying his kingdom from rocky outcrops, and you might spot the elegant chamois leaping across impossible slopes with ease. These two creatures, vaguely similar in appearance to mountain goats, are less frequently encountered and tend to live in the higher mountains in more secluded spots. You are more likely to come across them off the beaten path, close to the rock–vegetation line, but you might see them close at hand on a remote path. A herd of ibex are reported to spend a lot of time around the Pyramides Calcaires, away from the very busy Tour du Mont Blanc (TMB) in Val Veny. The chamois is an elusive resident, more likely to be seen at a distance on remote, high mountain slopes. They are much smaller than ibex and have distinctive small, curved horns.

Eagles and vultures soar in the skies and are not an infrequent sight. The eagle will keep a close eye on young grazing marmots, while the vulture is adept at 'cleaning up' the carcasses of both chamois and ibex that have fallen from high mountains

or which may have been caught in spring avalanches.

In the lower valleys you will encounter lizards of all shapes and colours lounging in the summer sun on walls and cliffs. On hot days basking adders may be encountered on paths; while they may be alarming to see, given time and space they will take cover.

A griffon vulture soars on the thermals (Route 21)

In the lower fields and pastures you will also come across a myriad of butterflies along with thousands of grasshoppers, which seem to make the ground move as you walk through.

PLANTS AND FLOWERS

The valleys covered in this guide offer the walker a vast range of climatic conditions for wildflowers. The lower slopes provide the ideal conditions for growing grapes for wine production; woodlands offer walnuts and hazelnuts galore; and the upper mountains allow the keen-eyed walker many opportunities to admire the abundance of wildflowers. Early summer is the optimum time to see the flowers in full bloom; to walk

19

through endless flower meadows is a true delight.

As the altitude increases so the range of flowers changes, with many growing only in the rocky environment of the Alps. A specialist book is recommended, such as Cicerone's *Alpine Flowers* by Gillian Price. Another useful identification guide is one of the many available apps that allow the user to identify flowers by colour and month.

Some commonly encountered flowers include:

- **Mountain or alpine aster** (*Aster alpinus*) looks like a large daisy with dyed-purple petals and can be found from 1400m to over 3000m.
- **Great masterwort** (*Astrantia major*) is an architecturally interesting plant commonly found in the lower mountains up to around 1800m.
- **Spring gentian** (*Gentiana verna*) is a highly protected deep-blue flower that grows at altitudes of up to 2700m.
- **Bearded bellflower** (*Campanula barbata*) is quite commonly found along the side of the path from 1000m to 3000m. The 'furry' flowers and distinctive flower shape help with

Clockwise from top left: mountain aster, great masterwort, spring gentian, bearded bell flower, arnica, alpenrose, golden rod, eyebright, glacial mouse ear martagon lily

identification. Both blue and white flowers are commonly found.

- **Bistort** (*Persicaria bistorta*) grows widely across the lower Alpine slopes up to an altitude of 3000m. Traditionally used to treat wounds and cuts, bistort is a member of the dock family.
- **Arnica** (*Arnica montana*) is both a poisonous and a protected species, growing at altitudes of up to around 2800m. Traditionally used as a medicinal herb, it is still used today. It can cause skin irritation on contact.
- **Golden Rod** (*Solidago virgaurea*), also known as woundwort, is a commonly found flowering plant with a long history of medicinal uses. As its alternative name suggests, it was used to treat wounds as well as kidney conditions. It works as an antiseptic, an astringent and a diuretic.
- **Alpenrose** (*Rhododendron ferrugineum*) is such a well-known Alpine bloom that almost every town will have a hotel or restaurant named after it. A sub-species of rhododendron, it blooms early and is often dying away by late July. It grows at altitudes of up to around 2300m.
- **Eyebright** (*Euphrasia*) was traditionally used to treat eye conditions such as conjunctivitis, as well as common ailments such as colds and hay fever. Recent

medical testing does not support the traditional herbal remedy claims.

- **Mountain houseleek** (*Sempervivum alpinum*) is a distinctive-looking plant found at mid to high altitudes, usually in damp spots. In traditional herbal remedies it was used to treat burns, warts, insect bites and stomach disorders.
- **Martagon Lily** (*Lilium martagon*), also known as the Turk's cap lily, is a protected species that grows at altitudes of approximately 2000m to 2400m. Its distinctive shape and height (up to 1m) make it easy to identify.
- **Wolf's bane** (*Aconitum vulparia*) is a protected species and highly poisonous. It was used to poison wolves and bears in times past. It should not be touched and there have been reports of people becoming ill from inhaling the pollen; admire it from a distance! It enjoys shaded spots high in the mountains at altitudes of up to around 2500m.
- **Alpine toadflax** (*Linaria alpina*) grows in the higher mountains, usually in gravelly terrain and above the vegetation line; as such it is a rare find and is likely to be found in small clumps near the highest cols.
- **Glacier mouse-ear** (*Cerastium alpinum*) is another 'rockery' plant that grows at mid to high altitudes.

- **Alpine rose** (*Rosa alpina*), not to be confused with Alpenrose, is a wild rose that is usually pink with a yellow-white heart.
- **Edelweiss** (*Leontopodium nivale*), a rare and protected flower, probably epitomises Alpine flowers like no other. Traditionally, it represents devotion or dedication and was a symbol of the resistance to Nazism in Germany. Today it is often used as a decoration in restaurants and as an emblem symbolising the Alps.

As you can imagine, many of these flowers are rare, often enjoying stringent legal protection. Some of these plants are irritants or even harmful to touch. Enjoy them from a distance, take photographs but leave them to grow and prosper in their natural environment.

Other regularly occurring wayside plants of interest include the 'fruits of the forest': tiny alpine strawberries, as well as raspberries and blackberries, often seen growing by the sides of paths.

A higher altitude fruit is the *mirtillo* (French: *myrtille*), which is a small, almost black, blueberry. It is common in parts of the UK and is known by a number of names, including whortleberry and bilberry.

If 'wayside snacking' is to be enjoyed, it is essential that the fruits are clearly identified, as other berries also grow along the wayside, not all of which are edible.

WEATHER

The Lys valley is on the very edge of the Alps with fine views to Piedmont in the mornings. As the Italian plain heats up each day, the air rises and meets the cooler air of the mountains, causing considerable cloud formation. It is usual for the afternoons to be cloudy and it is common to encounter mist or fog. The following morning (and possibly the evening before) clear skies are common, and you will be treated to far-reaching views once more.

The usual Alpine weather cycle is also to be expected: warm days developing into thunderstorms in the late afternoon. This is not usually a daily event but tends to develop over a few days and then resets. Early starts are always a good plan; to be sat enjoying a coffee and some well-earned cake is far more preferable than a late start and a drenching in a thunderstorm!

The normal walking season is from early July until mid September. Snow can lie on the ground until late June and can also fall overnight by mid August (although it tends to melt quite quickly in the morning). Old snow can lie in shaded hollows at higher altitudes, even in the height of summer, and should be treated with care. It is likely to be hard and slippery, the surface will be sprinkled with small stones and grit and a slide can cause nasty grazes and cuts.

Early and late in the season will see a cold start to the day, and snow of up to 150mm has even been experienced in mid September at the moderate altitudes of 1500m. In the middle of summer, the temperature can climb to over 30°C in the lower valleys during the middle of the day. A slightly chilly early morning, requiring a light fleece, followed by afternoon temperatures in the mid 20s is more

Descending from Rifugio Bonatti; an afternoon storm is brewing (Route 29)

typical in the high mountains during August. Early and late season walkers may well find it chillier in the mornings and after sundown.

HISTORY

The might of the Roman Empire defeated local tribes and, to protect the route through the Alps to Gaul, Augusta Praetoria Salassorum (Aosta), a large Roman military town, was established. Extensive remains can be found in the valley, notably in Aosta and lower down the valley in Donnas, where a section of the original Roman road is still evident running alongside the modern road.

Hannibal is thought by some to have crossed the Alps via the Great St Bernard Pass, but this remains one of the great archaeological mysteries: which pass did he use? Little conclusive evidence has yet been found to substantiate the claims made by the communities living in and around the great Alpine passes. The description by Roman historian Livy can be read to fit the Great St Bernard Pass; although the Petit St Bernard Pass (to the south) is deemed as being more likely in other accounts; both would have been known crossing points in those times.

Aosta was an important city of the Duchy of Savoy, second only to the capital cities of Chambéry and Turin. The Aosta coat of arms is centred around the Savoyard shield: a red field with a white cross extending

Ancient ways through historic streets, Cretaz (Route 13)

to the edges. Around the turn of the 19th century, the Duchy spread from Sardinia to the shores of Lac Léman. Many of the impressive fortresses date from this period and the House of Savoy was instrumental in the unification of Italy.

The formidable Forte di Bard is a must-see destination. Built at a narrowing of the valley upon a rock dome, it commands a narrow defile, meaning that whoever commanded the fort commanded the valley. It was deemed impregnable and withstood a two-week siege before finally succumbing to a cunning flanking manoeuvre via a steep track (Route 2) by the 40,000 troops under Napoleon's command in May 1800.

The town of Bard, at the foot of the fort, is a warren of medieval streets, and the bullet-scored walls pay tribute to the fierce street fighting of those times. A short walk from Donnas along the old Roman road (Route 1) is a fantastic way of arriving at Bard, taking about 40min each way.

In 1861 the Kingdom of Italy was founded with Vittorio Emanuele II, the King of Savoy, at its head. His son Umberto became the second King of Italy and was succeeded by Vittorio Emanuele III, who abdicated in 1946 following a vote in favour of Italy becoming a republic. Vittorio Emanuele, son of the last king, was exiled and lived in Geneva until his return in 2002 following a review by the European Court of Human Rights.

Old laundry washing, Cretaz (Route 13)

He had to relinquish any claim to the title 'King of Italy' and to ownership of the crown jewels (held in the national bank in Rome and estimated to be worth 2.5€ billion).

There is still some dispute over who is the 'real' King of Savoy; both the Duke of Aosta (Prince Amedeo) and the Prince of Naples (Vittorio Emanuele) lay claim to the throne and both have some justification to their claims. This dispute came to a head in 2004 at the wedding banquet of the King of Spain's son. It is reported that after the banquet Vittorio Emanuele punched Prince Amedeo twice in the face. First aid was provided by the Queen of Greece, and King Carlos was reported to have been livid!

These days, thanks to modern developments and the autonomous status of the Valle d'Aosta, the valley has a thriving economy. The ski holiday explosion of the 1960–1970s gave Courmayeur, Aosta and the valleys a new lease of life. The subsequent ski holiday infrastructure evident in the region created a vast number of jobs and career opportunities for the local population.

ART AND CULTURE

The Aosta valley has a rich and varied cultural heritage, and there is a feeling of great pride within the valley which celebrates its mountain roots through a range of festivals and events all summer long.

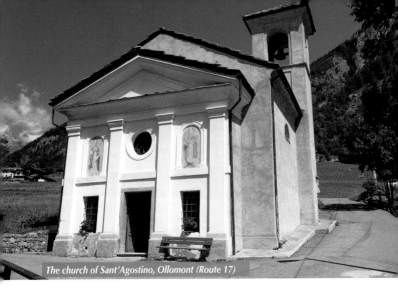
The church of Sant'Agostino, Ollomont (Route 17)

As a principal city of the House of Savoy, Aosta has a strong cultural identity. The arts are celebrated within the town throughout the year, with cultural events taking place throughout the summer; the most efficient way to find out what is currently happening is by visiting the valley's website, www.lovevda.it.

A religious influence is central to many events; every village and most hamlets have well-preserved, ancient churches, chapels or shrines. The adornment of even the simplest chapel is breathtaking and always worth taking a moment to explore.

Traditional dress is also a feature of village life on festival days, and visitors may well encounter women and girls dressed in long, black dresses with elaborate headwear during Assumption Day celebrations on 15 August, a national holiday. There are also parades of mountain guides in traditional dress on this day, Courmayeur being particularly notable. It is common for the local *bureau des guides* to host a celebration of all things mountainous during this week.

TRAIL RUNNING

The Aosta valley has a vibrant trail-running scene, thanks in no small part to the Ultra-Trail du Mont Blanc (UTMB). This world-famous race, which is around 171km long, begins in Chamonix and follows the TMB route, passing through Courmayeur at the approximate halfway point.

The Aosta valley is home to, arguably, the toughest race of all, the Tor des Géants (TDG). This phenomenal undertaking follows the Alta Via 2

(AV2) and then the Alta Via 1 (AV1) as a continuous loop of 330km with over 24,000m of ascent. However, in 2020 an even tougher race was planned, the Tor des Glaciers. These two races, combined with the UTMB, make Courmayeur the destination for trail runners.

Many of the routes in this guide make great courses for the experienced trail runner. The Walser villages walk (Route 9) is a substantial part of the 20km route that forms the trail-running weekend held in late July in Gressoney-Saint-Jean.

Below is a selection of other trail runs in the valley.

Monterosa Walser Trail Festival, Gressoney

Starting from the centre of Gressoney-Saint-Jean, with races covering a range of distances (including the 'Eco-Trail', a non-competitive 20km walk), this festival is a great weekend with a friendly atmosphere and something for every runner. The village has plenty to do for non-competitors too, varying from short walks to museums and Castel Savoia, www.monterosawalsertrail.com.

- 114km event: 8200m ascent; 40hr time limit
- 50km event: 4000m ascent; 15hr time limit
- 20km event: 850m ascent; 8hr time limit; open to over 16s
- 4.2km event: 200m ascent; reserved for families, children and people with disabilities

Trail 5 Colli, Lillianes

Located further dower down the Lys valley from Gressoney-Saint-Jean, this event comprises two routes, the longer being a 47km route (3900m ascent), which promises to be a challenge with, as the name implies, five cols to cross. The shorter course, an 'initiation', is 18km but is no pushover with 1700m of ascent. At present the race website is not operational. There is a Facebook site for the event, which usually takes place in mid July. It appears to have become a biannual event in recent years but, at the time of writing, Covid has had an impact on planning.

UYN Vertical, Courmayeur

This is a different type of race, a vertical km, meaning it is an uphill race with an altitude difference of 1000m. Part of a series of races along the length of the valley, this event takes place in late July. The distance is considerably further! Starting in the centre of Courmayeur, it finishes at the Pavilion station of Skyway Mont Blanc. There is a children's event and an even more challenging 2000m event, which continues to the old Helbronner hut, www.verticalcourmayeurmontblanc.com.

Tor X Series, Courmayeur

This has become the race to complete for serious Alpine trail runners, but recently it has gained a big brother: the Tor des Glaciers. There are two smaller siblings too; the Tot Dret is probably a perfect introduction to Alpine ultra-trail running. The baby brother, Passage au Malatrà, offers an introduction to Alpine trail running in a one-day event.

- Tor 450: Tor des Glaciers: 450km; 32,000m ascent; 190hr time limit
- Tor 330: Tor des Géants: 330km; 24,000m ascent; 150hr time limit
- Tor 130: Tot Dret: 130km; 12,000m ascent; 44hr time limit (qualifying race for the TDG)
- Tor 30: Passage au Malatrà: 30km; 2300m ascent; 8hr time limit

For more information, visit https://torxtrail.com/en/content/tor-des-géants®

Matterhorn Ultra Race

A new race for 2021, the Matterhorn Ultra Race is 182km and has over 12,000m of ascent. Beginning in Breuil-Cervinia, this could become a classic race, www.cervinomatterhornultrarace.it.

New events are cropping up all the time. Social media pages for the above events usually indicate whether they are part of a series and also promote other events throughout the valley and throughout the summer – no wonder the local runners are so fit! A good starting point is www.tourtrailvda.com.

Training camps are also being set up all the time offering specific training for races such as the UTMB and TDG.

Trekking

In addition to trail runs, there are also numerous trekking options in the region, principally sections of the AV1. (For full details of this trek, see the author's Cicerone guidebook, *The Giants' Trail*.)

The Tour du Mont Blanc (TMB) enters Italy at Col de la Seigne and leaves at Grand Col Ferret having followed the lengths of Val Veny and Val Ferret. Routes 27,28,29,30 and 31 share parts of the TMB and will mean we rub shoulders with the trekkers taking on what is probably the most popular trek in the Alps.

Pilgrims and trekkers on the Via Francigena, the ancient route from Canterbury to Rome, may also be encountered in the region. Many will tackle the route in one or two week sections over many years, others may be embarking on the entire journey over a few months. At over 2000km it is a significant journey.

The GTA (Grande Traversata delle Alpi) is another long distance trek that takes in parts of the eastern valleys. Not as well known, it is none-the-less a formidable undertaking, covering some 1000km.

For a delightful short trek, follow the AV1 from Donnas to Etoile du Berger, then to Rifugio Coda and on to Rifugio Barma, continuing on to Niel; a two-hour path returns to the valley floor. Alternatively, another full day on the AV1 takes you to Gressoney-Saint-Jean.

There are also a number of shorter treks, such as the Tour des Six which links six mountain huts in the eastern part of the range. The Sentieri del Lys has a number of options for supported trekking in the Lys valley, with luggage transfer included (see www.visitmonterosa.com for further details).

PLACES OF INTEREST

There may be some days when the weather has taken a turn or you fancy a day to visit places of interest. Plenty of options are available along the length of the valley. Leaflets and adverts abound in most of the accommodation, and local tourist information offices can be helpful too. Some venues worth considering include:

- **Forte di Bard**: this enormous fortress situated in the lower part of the valley is easily accessible from the motorway and will provide a full day's entertainment. With permanent and temporary exhibitions celebrating and explaining its history, the fort has something to keep everyone engaged. The Museum of the Alps provides an insight into Alpine life, while the artisan shops offer local, handmade crafts. A pleasant restaurant and café offer refreshments, and a picnic can be eaten in the open spaces. The fort and village beneath were used as film sets for *Avengers: Age of Ultron*, and full-size statues of the film's character are popular with younger members of the family, www.fortedibard.it.

- **Castel Savoia**: a fairy-tale castle built for Queen Margherita sits above Gressoney-Saint-Jean and is open to the public (check opening times via the local tourist office before visiting). With extensive alpine gardens and a striking appearance, it is a sight to behold. As was the fashion of the time, royal families would make trips to the mountains to enjoy the fresh mountain air: Margherita visited Castel Savoia as Victoria visited Balmoral. Her love of the mountains was profound and on 18 August 1893 she even climbed Punta Gnifetti (4554m), part of the Monte Rosa chain visible at the head of the valley.

- **Aosta**: as well as the street markets and shops, the extensive Roman remains are interesting to explore, along with short exploration walks which can be downloaded from the city's website. The museum provides a fascinating insight into the Roman era and the theatre is an impressive structure, often used as a backdrop for cultural events. For those with a fascination for archaeological remains, the Area Megalitica di Saint-Martin-de-Corléans is a must-see place. Mountain biking is a growing summer sport, and Pila's lift system can be accessed from Aosta, allowing a range of mainly downhill routes to be enjoyed.

29

Local shops offer hire options and advice on routes to follow.

- **Chamonix**: A trip on the bus, or a short drive through the tunnel, Chamonix is probably the modern capital of the Alps. It can fulfil all your gear-shopping dreams; towards the end of July all the shops have a huge clear-out sale aimed at the French holiday market. There is also an interesting museum in the centre of town.

  It is feasible to travel to Chamonix via the cable cars from Courmayeur, a truly spectacular way to arrive! A circular driving route returning via Col des Montets and Martigny (where there is a kennel and museum of St Bernard dogs) and across the Great St Bernard Pass makes for an enjoyable sightseeing route.

- **Lac Léman**: after travelling over the Great St Bernard Pass, you can enjoy a day on the enormous Lac Léman. There is no shortage of interesting places to visit, including the late-1800s splendour of Evian les Bains, a spa town and home to the famous bottled water; a small museum explains the process of sourcing and bottling the water. Music lovers will enjoy a visit to Montreux with its modern artistic flair. The lakeside statue of Freddie Mercury and the Queen Studio Experience (www.mercuryphoenixtrust.com) are popular destinations for fans. Château de Chillon (www.chillon.ch) is a fascinating walled castle, the setting for the 'Prisoner of Chillon' by Lord Byron, who scratched his name on the dungeon walls. Lausanne is the home to the International Olympic Committee and its museum, TOM (the Olympic Museum), www.olympic.org/museum. Steamers sail across the water, providing visitors with a different way of travelling around the lake.

- **Courmayeur**: the small town of Courmayeur is a pretty place; pedestrianised streets encourage visitors to wander. A range of shops sell souvenirs, local produce and outdoor equipment. There is a small museum in the Società delle Guide which chronicles the developments in mountaineering and allows a lot of hands-on experience of old equipment. Towards the lower part of the town is the bus station and the largest crampons in the world! Gondola lifts take visitors to Plan Chécrouit, where the open-air swimming pool, cafés and restaurants are popular when the valley feels too hot.

- **Skyway Monte Bianco**: having featured in *Kingsman: The Golden Circle*, this cable car, situated at Entrèves at the head of the valley, a few kilometres from Courmayeur (www.montebianco.com), is a must for any movie fans. It takes visitors to three stations, culminating in the Punta Helbronner at 3466m. With museums, visitor centres and restaurants at the various stations, it is far more than a sightseeing trip. It is also possible to visit Chamonix via the Vallee Blanche lift system which links Pte Helbronner to Aiguille du Midi. This is not without cost but will undoubtedly make for a day to remember as you are whisked over the snow and ice of the glaciers below.

- **Great St Bernard Monastery**: located at 2469m, the monastery will literally take your breath away. There has been a building here welcoming visitors and travellers for close to 1000 years and the tradition continues today. A museum and kennels explain the development and services of the monastic order, while the chapel and treasury provide an insight into the peace and reverence of the setting. The kennels offer accompanied walks with the dogs, as well as demonstrations of the dogs' training and breed development. Restaurants and cafés serve a range of local produce, while on the Italian side of the border the remains of the Roman road and temple foundations can be found. A short walk around the lake is popular, taking approximately an hour. Take a jumper as it is colder than might be expected this high above the valley floor.

Aosta sits at the relatively low altitude of 583m but is surrounded by some of the highest mountains in Europe. It has a warm climate but the high mountains hold snow long into the summer. Lower-level walks can be enjoyed in early April but much of the mid- to high-level walking will be inaccessible until late June. The Great St Bernard Pass doesn't open until late June and closes again in early October, although the road tunnel maintains year-round vehicle access.

The Italian holiday season is from early August until shortly after 15 August (Assumption Day), which is a national holiday (in France and Switzerland too). Accommodation is

Crossing late-season snow above Rifugio Elisabetta Soldini (Route 31)

31

at a premium during this period, but there are more events and attractions during this high season.

Early in the summer the *alpages* (alpine pastures) are carpeted with wildflowers and are a sight to behold. Snow may be lying on the higher ground and each day brings summer a little closer. Late August and September are also wonderful times; the crowds have dissipated, there is a nip in the air and the first hints of autumn are visible; wild fruit and nuts can be foraged and the valley hotels are out of high-season prices. But beware, some of the restaurants begin to close down in the second half of September.

ACCESS AND TRAVEL

Most visitors will probably drive and a car is of great value in the area as it allows easier travel around and between the valleys. It is feasible to travel from the UK and arrive in the valley by late afternoon if travelling by air, and within two days if driving. With access to modern, fast trains, travelling by rail is another realistic option.

By train: Turin is accessible by train from many European cities; the TGV service from Paris is probably a favourable option for many travellers. From Turin there are regular trains into the Aosta valley, usually changing in Ivrea.

By air: Turin is the nearest airport. There are regular train and bus routes from Turin, most of which change in Ivrea. Trains to Aosta, and stations lower in the valley, are regular – roughly hourly.

By car: The journey from northern Europe can be a treat in itself, either via Besançon and Switzerland and over the Great St Bernard Pass or via Chamonix and the Mont Blanc Tunnel. Both have merits and offer different views and opportunities.

The tunnels through the Great St Bernard Pass and Mont Blanc are quite expensive (48CHF and €59 returns, respectively, in 2021). The road over the Great St Bernard Pass is open during the summer and adds about 30 minutes to the journey along with the option to visit the monastery.

Following Brexit, the need for additional paperwork to drive abroad must not be overlooked by British travellers.

Locally, there are a few bus services which may be of use. Generally, they run up and down the valleys in the mornings and afternoons, starting and terminating at the main Aosta valley town at the mouth of the valley. The main operators are Arriva Italia (https://aosta.arriva.it) and SVAP (www.svap.it) and prices compare to those in the UK. It appears that new timetables are only produced when there is a timetable change, hence the most recent timetable may be dated 2016 or even earlier.

Private taxis may be a viable alternative for groups; they are much more expensive than the buses but will allow travellers greater flexibility and can reduce the transfer time considerably. For example, Aosta to Saint-Rhémy-en-Bosses will cost around €50, while a bus will be about €4–6 per person.

Some support is available in the eastern valleys in the form of TrekBus, which offers very reasonably priced links within the Gressoney, Ayas and Valtournenche valleys. To book call +39 348 4458175. The TrekBus service runs in the early morning and late afternoon and must be booked at least the day before.

It is important to be aware of travel restrictions and requirements for entry into Italy. In recent times this has not been as straightforward as previously, particularly in relation to cumulative visit duration in Schengen Area countries and Covid related restrictions. Health and Covid advice, mountain safety and general safety information can be found at www.gov.uk/foreign-travel-advice/italy.

ACCOMMODATION

The Aosta valley has a long history of catering for travellers' needs, and there is no shortage of options for every budget. Hotels and a range of B&B options exist in most villages in the valleys and can be researched easily online; alternatively, see

The unusual yurt accommodation at Rifugio Champillon (Route 22)

www.aosta-valley.co.uk for links to accommodation throughout the area.

Campsites are not as numerous as in other parts of Europe but some well-equipped sites do exist. It is advisable to book in the height of summer and to request a shaded spot, if possible, as the sun can be strong.

The mountain *rifugio* (refuge) is an experience in which to savour a real adventure. They provide a basic but welcome night's sleep, traditional food and very good locations in the heart of the mountains. Some are owned by the Italian Alpine Club (CAI), while others are privately owned, usually by local farming families.

A number of the routes in this guide include a mountain refuge, so it is perfectly feasible to add a night in a refuge to your holiday experience. When the crowds depart after their lunch and the trekkers arrive, there is a certain camaraderie between those staying. Watching the sun set behind a myriad of mountain peaks is a humbling experience. Daylight fades, the temperature falls and the delicious aromas of dinner beckon.

In high summer prior booking is highly recommended, either via email in advance or by phone a day or so ahead (village tourist offices and hotels can help with this). Should your plans change it is also expected that you cancel your booking, otherwise the guardian may well refuse other bookings or even initiate an expensive search and rescue as they will be anxiously expecting your arrival.

A certain code of conduct is expected of hut users. Most are common sense but failure to adhere to them may earn the miscreant a quick rebuke from the guardian.

- Trekking poles should be left in the porch
- Boots are stored in the entrance area and 'hut slippers' should be worn indoors; they are stored in the boot storage area
- Inform the guardian of your arrival and register; guardians may want a formal document, such as a passport
- You will usually then be shown to your dormitory where a bed may be designated. Spread your sheet sleeping bag on your bed to indicate it is taken

Rifugio Elisabetta Soldini and the Mont Blanc massif (Routes 30 and 31)

- A basket or cubby hole to store personal items is commonly available, as well as a shelf near the head end of the bed/bunk. Keep a headtorch at hand; lighting in a hut is often limited and weak as it is also solar sourced
- Damp items can be placed in the drying room or spread out in the sun (once the sun sets the temperature will drop quickly)
- The guardian will usually ask where you are travelling on to and may offer a suitable breakfast time taking this into account
- A running tab will be kept for additional drinks and snacks and settling up will often be after dinner
- It is expected that payment will be made in cash in huts
- As everything is flown in and out, it is also expected that any personal rubbish is taken with you

CLOTHING

Alpine walking does not require any particularly specialist equipment other than comfortable, warm and waterproof clothing. It is likely that most mid-summer walking will be in T shirts and shorts but it is important that clothing is carried for inclement weather. A warm layer and waterproof clothing along with supportive footwear are recommended.

You will see many European travellers favouring a poncho over full waterproofs. This is a debatable point; a poncho is cheap, often less than €30, and packs up to quite a small package. It allows more ventilation and most have a 'hunch' to accommodate a backpack. The downside is that it does not provide full cover and will flap about a lot in high winds.

Appendix C provides a recommended kit list and advice on appropriate equipment.

Via ferratas will require stiff footwear and gloves are a sensible consideration. Obviously, full via ferrata equipment is obligatory, including a helmet, harness and via ferrata lanyard to latest standards; a full list can be found in the above appendix.

FOOD AND DRINK

Food production is celebrated in every valley; a range of local produce is usually available and is worth tasting. Great pride is taken in the local cheeses and dried meat sausages, all widely available and perfect for lunch packs. A common offering is *taglieri* (a cheese or meat platter), while polenta cooked with *fontina* (a local cheese) is another regularly encountered speciality.

Local drinks include a range of beers, wines and fruit-based drinks, but one you will repeatedly encounter is *grappa*, a strong spirit made from grapes. As it uses the skin, seeds and pulp of grapes as its base constituents, it is not too difficult to see how it is a by-product of the wine industry.

A feast at Adler's Nest, Above Staffal, Lys Valley (Route 11)

The table and bench on the descent path make a fine lunch stop (Route 21)

A wooden container called a *grolla* is often seen in many shops and restaurants. It is a multi-spouted drinking container that is passed around the table after dinner. It contains *café de l'amité* (coffee of friendship), a strong, black coffee in which spirits are blended, often *génépi*. The *grolla* is believed to have begun life as a wooden clog shared between shepherds.

LANGUAGE

As would be expected, the first language of the region is Italian but, given the Savoyard roots of the region, French is also widely spoken. English is less likely to be encountered in the mountains, although the main valley settlements often have staff who can speak English.

An attempt in Italian or French is warmly received and even the most basic efforts will be encouraged and appreciated.

Appendix B provides some basic phrases to assist you, but a small comprehensive phrase book is a worthwhile addition.

MAPS AND NAVIGATION

Italian cartography varies; some maps have inaccuracies and are of limited use for fine navigation. However, the 1:25,000 Carta dei Sentieri by L'Escursionista Editore are of a good standard, are recommended by some of the guide associations in the valleys

and have GPS compatibility. The maps are also available from the publisher as a digital download for either Android or iPhone from its website: www.escursionistaeditore.com

The maps are printed on a waterproof material, cost around €10 each and are sold in numerous shops in the valleys, but usually the range is limited to the valley you are visiting. Shops in Aosta tend to sell maps for the entire valley. They are also available to purchase online with international postage from the website above.

1:25,000 Carta dei Sentieri by L'Escursionista Editore
* 12: Basse valli d'Ayas e del Lys
* 08: Monte Rosa – Alte valli d'Ayas e de Lys
* 07: Valtournenche, Monte Cervino
* 06: Valpelline, Saint-Barthélemy
* 05: Gran San Bernardo – Valle di Ollomont
* 01: Monte Bianco, Courmayeur

The 1:50,000 maps by Instituto Geografico Centrale are of limited use; contours are set at 50m intervals, meaning much detail is lost, and there is no GPS compatibility.

Other maps are available locally at a range of scales, but the 1:25,000 maps from L'Escursionista Editore are the most comprehensive.

WAYMARKING

It is almost universal to use red and white flashes to mark paths in the

Commonly found signs along the way: The triangle of the Alta Via 1; arrow indicators on rocks, two signs on one path to the same place with a range of differences: names, times, altitudes.

Western Alps; however, the forestry commission in the Aosta region also uses red and white flashes, therefore paths here are marked with yellow flashes.

Most path junctions have signposts indicating the destination of the path, its altitude and the expected time to walk there. Not as common in the Alps is the Italian practice of numbering paths (1, 2, 3, etc.) and adding a sub-division (A, B, C, etc.). The timings are generally accurate but can occasionally have discrepancies. There may also be minor variations in spelling and whether 'de', 'del' or 'della' is included or not.

Other navigational considerations are the signs for popular running events in the valleys and the barely comprehensible TDG, a 330km race that compresses the AV1 and AV2 into a one-week event for ultra-runners. To walk this route would take over a month; the winners complete it in an unimaginable 70 hours or less!

SAFETY AND EMERGENCIES

The universal European emergency number (112) can be used to contact the local emergency services. Do not expect the call handler to be able to speak English, although this may be the case. Be prepared to speak basic Italian or French; composing a phrase or two on paper before making the call may well help. Make sure you can explain where you are and what has happened. Most, but not all, rescues and recoveries will be by helicopter and, therefore, adequate insurance is essential. Make sure any policy covers helicopter evacuation.

In an emergency situation

- Keep out of the weather – some sort of survival bag, or preferably a bothy bag, will make life substantially more comfortable while waiting for help to arrive
- Keep everyone warm – use spare clothes, huddle together in a bothy bag, put on a hat and gloves early (before the heat has been lost)
- Insulate yourself from the ground – use a small mat or spare equipment to keep off the cold ground
- Make yourselves visible – torches, bright clothing and a suitably visible position will help the rescuers locate the group
- Keep your mobile phone on and free from other traffic – the emergency services may want to call you back. Ensuring adequate phone battery life is also essential; turn off non-essential apps and other power-consuming aspects of your phone

INSURANCE

It is advisable to be insured for mountain walking and other activities. The Global Health Insurance Card (GHIC) is the replacement for the European Health Insurance Card (EHIC) and is a free card that provides the bearer with basic health care – but it is not an insurance policy. Many insurance providers expect clients to have an EHIC or GHIC. To apply for a card, visit www.gov.uk/global-health-insurance-card.

The insurance policy must cover the activities being undertaken; a growing number of insurance providers now offer cover for mountain and adventure sports. The British Mountaineering Council (BMC) offers a comprehensive scheme for members, which is particularly competitive for those with pre-existing medical conditions and for older trekkers (basic membership of the BMC is a

requirement). The Austrian Alpine Club (AAC) provides some cover as part of its basic membership package (be aware that this is not a comprehensive policy and does not cover travel to and from the mountains). Snowcard offers a customisable policy and provides a discount for second members at the same address. Endsleigh offers very good options, including cover for groups. Its policies can also be customised to cover other activities beyond trekking; it is important to ensure that the higher altitude option is included (to cover altitudes of up to 3000m).

Annual policies often offer considerable savings if you are planning more than two trips abroad.

USING THIS GUIDE

This guidebook describes 32 routes, arranged by geographical location within the valley. Two of these routes

Climbing to Fenêtre de Tsignanaz (Route 14)

(Routes 26 and 32) are technically via ferratas (see below).

Most of the routes follow reasonably frequented paths and although the surface is uneven and rocky in places, it is not too challenging. Several are considered 'protected walks', which means they feature permanent structures (foot plates, handrails, etc.) to help protect the walker. Any walk that features more exposure than might be expected will have some form of protection, probably fixed ropes as handrails. In these instances, those unsure about the exposure may choose to make use of a couple of slings and karabiners.

In this guidebook the grading for each walk is as follows:

- Grade 1: a simple path with a moderate gradient, suitable for all walkers
- Grade 2: a reasonably strenuous Alpine walk, typical of a day in the mountains; usually 5–7 hours in duration
- Grade 3: some technical sections where previous Alpine experience will be advantageous. Grade 3 may also be used to indicate particularly long days (over eight hours) that will be physically demanding.

The CAI and local Valle d'Aosta councils' grades closely correlate:

- T: tourist path – a very well-marked, gentle path, usually limited to the valley bottom
- E: trekking path – the usual features of a mountain path will be present without technical difficulties or challenges
- EE: expert hikers – steep or exposed paths may be encountered, and the ground may be more technical. Sections may be protected with fixed-rope handrails and the occasional footstep attached to rock outcrops. Steep rocky sections of path may be encountered for short distances

Two routes (Routes 26 and 32) touch on the edge of the International Climbing and Mountaineering Federation (UIAA) grades. These will be graded 'Facile' and are, therefore, at the very beginning of the mountaineering spectrum. They require mountain knowledge and some decision-making in terms of routes and safety. Ice axes, crampons and ropes would not normally be needed on these routes. However, an experienced and prudent mountain walker will probably carry a short rope and maybe a couple of slings and karabiners to use as protection on short sections of the route for less experienced members of the group.

Estimating times is always a challenge. The times given in this guidebook are, generally, those advised on signposts with real life experience tempering them on occasions.

As walkers get fitter, more acclimatised and more familiar with the terrain, it is normal to find that they begin to move quicker than the standard time given on signposts. Corrective panels over original times show they are open to variation and interpretation. The times given in this guidebook are based on the author's own experience and are walking times, so do not include rests and breaks, which may add an hour or two to a day, particularly when there's a lot to see!

Via ferrata

Via ferrata routes are a developing mountain sport and have their roots in the defences built in the Italian Dolomites during World War 1. Modern routes have no such history; they are built and promoted purely for sporting and leisure purposes. They take different lines up and along the cliffs and ridges of the mountains and generally require

you to attach yourself to embedded infrastructure via a specific self-belay device. Sporting routes will take vertical or overhanging lines for maximum adrenalin adventure, while other routes take a more moderate line and are often protected routes to access mountain refuges.

There are a range of via ferratas scattered along the length of the Aosta valley, from those suitable for children to a stupendously steep route that claims to be the hardest in Italy.

Do not hesitate to hire a qualified guide if you are in any doubt. This can be done at any tourist information office (TIC) in the valley. (Similarly, TICs and *bureaux des guides* offer guided via ferrata trips for those without the equipment or experience

VIA FERRATA GRADES

In the Aosta area an adaptation of the Alpine grading system has been adopted. These bear a resemblance to those used for mountaineering and follow the same sequence.

- F (Facile): straightforward beginners' routes or paths with protection in place.
- PD (Peu Difficile): straightforward routes designed to encourage newcomers.
- AD (Assez Difficile): more challenging and steeper routes requiring previous experience.
- D (Difficile): harder routes demanding fitness and previous experience. Vertical or short overhanging sections will be encountered and significant exposure can be expected.
- TD (Très Difficile): extended vertical or overhanging sections will be encountered.
- ED (Extrême Difficile): Sustained routes requiring stamina, balance and strength throughout.

The path snakes its way to Colle di Carisé (Route 4)

to take part independently.) Where equipment is needed, this is included in the route description. Equipment can be hired or purchased from various TICs and outdoor shops in the valley. See Appendix C for more info.

The one route in this guide that has full via ferrata equipment, Route 32, is a well-equipped route. Anyone following it must be properly equipped and experienced, otherwise it can become very dangerous very quickly.

While the via ferrata section in Route 26 will be seen by most as a protected path, some might find the use of via ferrata equipment provides reassurance.

A number of via ferrata routes can also be downloaded from the Cicerone website (www.cicerone. co.uk/1015). These are summaries only and additional information and resources will be required before undertaking these routes. They are of the sporting variety and involve steep cliffs, exposed ledges and significant exposure. Escaping routes can be challenging and will certainly require a range of mountaineering and rock-climbing skills. Obviously, the appropriate equipment, skills and experience are required before attempting these without professional leadership.

Additional app support

There are some useful smartphone apps that can be used as a supplement to the information within this guidebook:

- Alpine flowers: 'The world of alpine flowersie' is an unusually titled but detailed app which allows for wildflower identification by colour and month of the year

Mont Blanc and the Val Veny from the summit of Mont de la Saxe (Route 28)

- Location: the majority of the routes are close enough to the Swiss border to be accessed on Swiss mapping, a free online service available at www.swisstopo. ch
- Weather: a commonly used and reliable app is 'yr.no' (a Norwegian website provided by the national meteorological and broadcasting services)
- A phrase book app is also a useful addition; if it is in French as well as Italian so much the better

GPX tracks

GPX tracks for the routes in this guidebook are available to download free at www.cicerone.co.uk/1015/GPX. If you have not bought the book through the Cicerone website, or have bought the book without opening an account, please register your purchase in your Cicerone library to access GPX and update information.

A GPS device is an excellent aid to navigation, but you should also carry a map and compass and know how to use them. GPX files are provided in good faith, but in view of the profusion of formats and devices, neither the author nor the publisher accepts responsibility for their use. We provide files in a single standard GPX format that works on most devices and systems, but you may need to convert files to your preferred format using a GPX converter such as gpsvisualizer. com or one of the many other apps and online converters available.

Looking down on Forte di Bard (Route 2)

MAIN VALLEY

The Aosta valley has many short walks along its length, as well as the 1700km Via Francigena, starting in Canterbury and finishing in Rome, which takes older, less travelled roads and tracks down the length of the valley and onwards. By using trains and/or buses it is possible to follow small sections of this historic route, but in the height of the summer, temperatures of 30°C in the valley are not unusual. The paths and tracks around Forte di Bard, however, are worthy of some exploration as they excel at providing footsteps through history.

Map: 1:25,000 Carta dei Sentieri by L'Escursionista Editore 12: Basse valli d'Ayas e del Lys.

ROUTE 1

Forte di Bard and the Roman road, Donnas

Start/Finish	Donnas library car park (underground, free)
Distance	4.5km
Ascent	30m
Descent	30m
Grade	1
Time	1hr 20min (round trip)

This short walk allows the visitor to experience a whole world of history in a day as well as offering an alternative way of approaching the popular Forte di Bard complex.

The arch on the Roman road is clearly visible when approaching Pont-Saint-Martin from the upper valley. The road is remarkably well preserved and the worn surface clearly shows evidence of cart and carriage wheels rolling along here for thousands of years. Being part of the Via Francigena, this walk is also part of the ancient pilgrim route to Rome from Canterbury. The dominating Forte di Bard is the destination, making it an historical exploration suitable for the whole family. As the setting for a recent Avengers film and a host of museums and exhibitions, the fort will easily take a full day of exploration. A host of artisan shops, cafés and restaurants in the old town are the icing on the cake.

It is worth considering that by the time the road from Canterbury to Rome was being trodden, the Roman road upon which this section is based would have been around a thousand years old.

From the centre of Donnas follow the road out of town in the direction of Bard (up the valley). At the junction approximately 50 metres after the library follow the road uphill signed 'strada romana; arco romano' for approximately 30 metres to the right.

Turn left (Path 103, which is the Via Francigena) into the medieval street and buildings of old Donnas **(5min)**. ◄

This narrow road has been paved in a traditional stone style at some considerable expense and begins by passing through an arch indicating the old town wall.

46

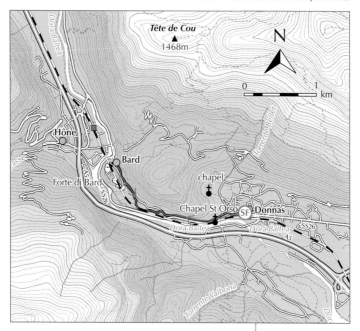

Continue down the road taking time to look at the buildings and some of the old signs painted above the doorways. ▸

At the end of the old street is the **Chapel of St Orso** which has existed for over 900 years and was built to provide protection from the frequent river floods (**15min**).

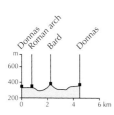

The Roman road is ahead; just how many wheels rolling along it would it have taken to create the ruts?

The road was called **'delle Gallia'** (of Gaul, modern day France) and was the

About 100 metres along the road, look out for the palace of the Enrielle family with its round tower. This building also housed travellers before it became a prison.

47

first road in the Aosta valley. To cut a roadway into solid rock is testament to the ingenuity and technological standards of the Roman engineers as well as the hard labour of the slaves who created such an impressive construction.

The 36 (XXXVI) milestone (a large column) indicates 36 Roman miles to Aosta.

Walk along this section of road; although only 221 metres in length it will probably take a while as there are many distractions to catch your eye. Pass through the remarkable **archway**. ◄

Continue along the obvious road, which is now a modern path, away from the busy road. Pass some vineyards until the surface changes to river pebbles set in concrete (**20min**).

The ancient archway on the Roman road, Donnas

48

Follow this to reach a track junction. At the time of writing the old road is closed here due to the risk of rock-fall from the cliffs above (**25min**).

Take the road left which descends quite steeply before contouring under the rock face and past some allotments. Climb steeply to regain the old road (**35min**).

Forte di Bard is visible ahead, follow the road into the beautifully preserved village of **Bard** (**40min**).

The small **open-air museum/ecology site** on the left makes for an interesting diversion. Glacial erratics, striations and other geological features can be discovered along with some ancient stone carvings which encircle the erratic boulder.

Bard has a number of small artisan shops and cafés/restaurants along its main street.

FORTE DI BARD

The complex of Forte di Bard is imposing; it is easy to see how it would have controlled travel in the valley, and the strategic importance of its situation is obvious.

There has been a fort of some description on the rocky promontory for over a thousand years, dating back to wooden palisades in the 5th century. The present buildings were constructed between 1830 and 1838 because Charles Albert of Savoy was worried about a French invasion.

The fort's troops were outnumbered 100:1 by Napoleon's Grande Armée, but thanks to its situation they successfully held off the army for two weeks as it attempted to invade Italy, having crossed the Great St Bernard Pass. His successful plan to bypass the fort by a difficult path resulted in vicious street fighting in the village of Bard. The bullet-pock-marked walls today provide ample evidence of the intensity of the street fighting that took place.

Advances in military technology meant the fort fell into disuse, and it was handed over to the local administration in the 1980s. Since then it has been developed to become the attraction it is today.

Permanent exhibitions include an Alpine museum and exhibitions on the fort's history. And with temporary exhibitions and displays of local artists' work, there is always something to see. The 2015 film *Avengers: Age of*

Ultron used the fort and the village as sets, and artefacts can be encountered around the site. Children can also partake in a virtual climb of Mont Blanc!

The Hotel Cavour (named after Camillo Benso, the Conte di Cavour, who was responsible for its development and who became Italy's first prime minister following unification in 1861) in the upper part of the fort is a unique place to stay. This part of the fort was originally the officers' and women's quarters; eleven rooms are available and are all equipped to a high standard. There is a small restaurant and a café within the complex offering lunchtime meals and refreshments.

The return is by the same route but allows different views throughout, and features that may have been missed on the outward journey will be spotted on the return leg (**1hr 20min**).

Forte di Bard from the Roman road

ROUTE 2
Napoleon's diversion
route

Start/Finish	Bard – parking available in the village of Hône (or at the fort complex)
Distance	9km
Ascent	640m
Descent	640m
Grade	2, a very small section of fixed rope aids a steep descent of no more than 5 metres
Time	3hr 45min

As Napoleon's power increased, his expansion across Europe seemed to show no bounds. He had famously crossed the Alps via the Great St Bernard Pass and was on the march into the Italian states. Nothing could stop him.

Then he encountered the Forte di Bard. The fort guarded a very narrow passage of the river, and the only road passed through the small village of Bard at the foot of the fort. After two weeks of a fruitless siege no further progress had been made. Then, after scouting the area, Napoleon and his army hatched an audacious plan: to bypass the fort via a steep climb and attack from the other side. This route follows their route.

The route begins opposite the footbridge from Hône, about 20 metres to the left after crossing the bridge. If parking at the fort, leave the car park and walk right from the entrance along the pavement to the bridge.

Take Path 2 'Albard di Bard' (confusingly marked as Path 1 on the Carta dei Sentieri 1:25,000 map). ▶ Pass to the right of a farmhouse to join a track (**20min**).

Follow this track to join a quiet road (**25min**). This road continues to climb gently to a road junction (**35min**).

The path is an old, well-worn staircase that climbs quite steeply between houses before entering shaded woodland.

51

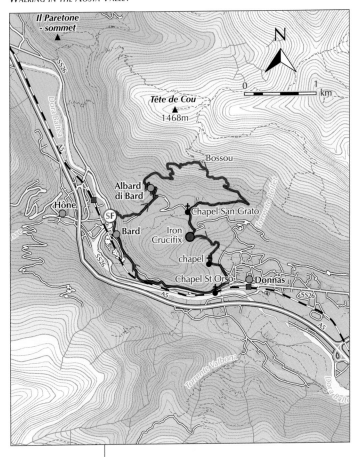

Be wary of signs indicating short cuts; some of these paths end abruptly with little to indicate which way to go.

Take the left fork and follow the road as it zigzags to the village of **Albard di Bard**, 643m (**55min**). ◄

The **village architecture** is very old, mostly drystone built. It is believed Napoleon stayed here during the siege and several properties have embrasures to allow musket fire.

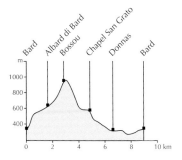

A sign indicates Path 1 to the right. Follow this path, a delightful walled track that winds its way through fields to join a road at a car park, 627m (**1hr**).

Napoleonic musket ball scars, Bard

53

Follow Path 1 to a junction which is reached in a couple of minutes. Take the right fork, still Path 1, and continue climbing to reach a wonderful viewpoint looking down to the fort and across to the mountains beyond (**1hr 15min**).

Follow the path as it winds its way up the hillside to reach a restored chalet at Chesal, 844m (**1h 30min**).

Keep climbing to reach the day's highpoint of the abandoned chalets of **Bossou**, 943m (**1hr 40min**). ◄

Pass through what appears to be the old 'street' of the settlement and within a few minutes you will reach a split in the path. A large stone indicates an inverse triangle symbol with a '3' inside it. This path is the descent (marked as Path 6 on the map). Follow this path to a well-built stone staircase and abandoned chalets at Fobe, 817m (**2hr**).

A minute or so later a small shrine offers a fabulous view of the valley and what is, in effect, the end of the Alps as the Italian plain stretches into the distance.

Continue along the path to join a track (**2hr 10min**).

Turn right on this track, downhill. Follow the track as it descends through the forest to become a road. Pass through the hamlet of Planet and keep following the road downhill to the small chapel of **San Grato** (**2hr 20min**).

Follow signs for Path 3 to the left along the road. After only three or four minutes a path leaves the road to the right; be sure to follow this as Path 3 signs will no longer be encountered. After only a minute or two the path bends rightwards and splits. Take the lower path (old red arrows on rocks) ◄ Follow the path as it descends to the right. It is steep at first but well used by local farmers. Pass a farm and then a very short section of rope helps you descend a steep section (**2hr 35min**).

Keep following the path, passing an information board, to arrive at a road and another small chapel (**2hr 50min**).

Follow the road downhill and at a junction take the right turn onto a rough farm track through the vineyards. Take another left at the end of the vine road to join a road (**3hr**).

These are worth a short exploration, particularly those built into the rock but, as always with abandoned buildings, care is needed.

An iron crucifix is a good waymarker here.

Old shop sign, Donnas

Follow this road down into **Donnas (3hr 05min)**.

From here, the return to **Bard** and Hône is along the Roman road (Route 1), which takes about 40 minutes **(3hr 45min)**.

LOWER LYS VALLEY

Sunset from the balcony at Rifugio Barma (Route 6)

The verdant lower Lys valley is sometimes overlooked by those making their way to the jewel of the valley, Gressoney-Saint-Jean; but to do so would be a shame, as the lower valley has a different character and a warmer climate due to its lower altitude.

There are plenty of trails wandering along the valley sides, twisting their way between fields and villages, following ancient mule tracks (*mulattiera*) towards the higher mountains. Beautiful arched bridges cross torrents and there's even an ancient gold mine hidden among the mountains. Chestnut orchards abound in the lower valley and the nuts are a feature of many local dishes.

The valley opens at Pont-Saint-Martin with its Roman single-span, arched bridge, to climb to Fontainemore and on to Issime, the administrative town for the lower valley, which offers the best range of services and shops, including a pharmacy and doctor's surgery as well as a police station.

The principal area to explore on foot is the mountains above Sassa. The Etoile du Berger at Sassa is hard to beat for value for money and a warm welcome, as well being the starting point for many walks. Home-cooked, local cuisine is a feature, and the tranquil restaurant terrace offers an engaging place to enjoy a drink at the end of a day's walking.

The mountain range includes the Mont Mars Nature Reserve and some secluded refuges.

Map: 1:25,000 Carta dei Sentieri by L'Escursionista Editore 12: Basse valli d'Ayas e del Lys.

ROUTE 3
Plan des Sorcières and Col Portola

Start/Finish	Etoile du Berger, Sassa
Distance	9km
Ascent	610m
Descent	610m
Grade	1+ to 2
Time	2hr 40min to 3hr 40min (depending on route chosen)

The view from the Col Portola is one that is usually only seen in the high mountains: sweeping slopes, rocky ridges with summits peeking out from the clouds and a mountain hut perched high above. Although only a short walk, it takes in a reasonable amount of altitude gain and attention to the route is required in one or two spots, hence the grading is closer to 2 than might be expected for a normal, 'simple' walk.

Passing through forests and alpages to reach an unusual plateau, reputed to have been home to witches (*sorcières*), we reach the fine viewpoint of Col Portola. With the pastures hosting an abundance of wildflowers, it is a truly delightful day.

Begin by following the road from the parking above the Etoile du Berger, 1376m, for about 150 metres until you reach a well-signed path on the left next to a small building set into the steep pastures. This path is signed for Col Portola and also Rifugio Coda. There are also small, square, red and white signs for the Trail 5 Colli pointing along the same path.

The **Etoile du Berger** takes its name from the local name for Venus, the first star seen in the evening sky and an indication to shepherds that it was time to make their way home, hence 'the shepherds' star'.

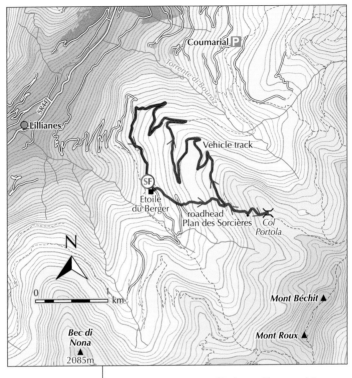

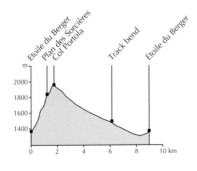

Climb steadily on a rising traverse, through pastures and a few isolated farm buildings, to cross a vehicle track twice and, as the ground becomes rockier, a few boulders strewn in the fields. The path becomes a little more indistinct here but is discernible. Laid rocks form the path near the buildings. Keep on the path to cross the **vehicle track** twice in close succession to cut the hairpin corner. This next rising traverse is about 250 metres long and ends at an important but indistinct junction. As the path meets a vehicle track be sure to identify and follow the path to Plan des Sorcières/Col Portola/Coda which takes a directly uphill route. End of vehicle track, 1810m (**1hr 10min**).

Care needs to be taken here, as there is another path which contours around the hillside to a lonely coombe (effectively the vehicle track continuing as a path) which can be accidentally followed. Some arrowed waymarking indicates this path but there is no marking for the Trail 5 Colli route. It is possible to explore this remote coombe by following the path which eventually peters out in the wild bowl, a tranquil and secluded spot, about 20 minutes each way.

Follow the path directly uphill to quickly gain height towards some well-kept buildings before trending rightward to reach the Plan des Sorcières, a small plateau.

There is a **large rock** on the left with ancient carvings that are reputed to represent Pleiades, a star cluster that is clearly visible with the naked eye; the stars are also referred to as the Seven Sisters, which may well be the origin of the 'witches' who

The Pleiades rock, Plan des Sorcières

were believed to have inhabited the remote plateau. Other rocks on the plateau also have cupola engravings and further support the theory that ancient rites were practised here.

Rifugio Coda is visible on the skyline and Mont Mars rises impressively behind it. The warm, protected slopes just beyond the col seem to be a perfect spot for early ripening mirtillo nero (myrtille in French), the commonly found wild blueberry.

Follow the path upwards to arrive at the col and an impressive view that opens out, **Col Portola**, 1966m (**1hr 40min**). ◄

From here there are two options: the first is to retrace the ascent route and return in about an hour. A longer alternative (approximately two hours) is to descend to the previously mentioned **roadhead** for the vehicle track and then follow this track rightwards. This descent is longer but is gentler on the knees and there is virtually no traffic on the track. This track descends in long sweeping loops to a hairpin where there is a path signed to Ponte Bouro. Keep on the track as it descends further and gradually becomes a road. It meets the 'main road' to Etoile du Berger and a short walk of about 10 minutes uphill on the road to return to the **Etoile du Berger** (**2hr 40min or 3hr 40min**).

The terrace of the Etoile du Berger – perfect for a relaxing evening

ROUTE 4

The Two Monts: Mont Roux and Mont Bechit

Start/Finish	Etoile du Berger, Sassa
Distance	10km
Ascent	1030m
Descent	1030m
Grade	2 – maps indicate via ferrata but this is a protected path
Time	5hr 15min

These two mountain summits, both over 2300m in altitude, are the high points on a rolling mountain ridge that offers far-reaching views and an atmospheric situation when the afternoon mists roll across them. Part of the AV1, the ridge is well trodden but never likely to be busy and gives a feeling of the high mountains without being overly exposed. You may well spot mountain goats keeping an eye on your progress from the upper slopes of Mont Bechit. Any slightly exposed parts of the path benefit from fixed lines and an occasional metal footplate. The route can be tackled in either a clockwise or an anti-clockwise direction (the directions given here are for a clockwise circuit but both routes are equally enjoyable). Rifugio Coda lies about 25 minutes from Col de Carisé, allowing for a morning coffee or afternoon tea.

The first objective for the day is Col Portola, 1966m (Route 3). Begin by following the road from the parking above the **Etoile du Berger**, 1376m, for about 150 metres until you reach the well-signed path. Follow this uphill to cross an **vehicle track** twice and, as the ground becomes rockier, a few boulders strewn in the fields. The path becomes a little more indistinct here but, with care, it is discernible. Keep on the path and cross the vehicle track twice in close succession to cut the hairpin corner. As the path meets a vehicle track be sure to identify the path to Plan des Sorcières/Col Portola/Coda which takes

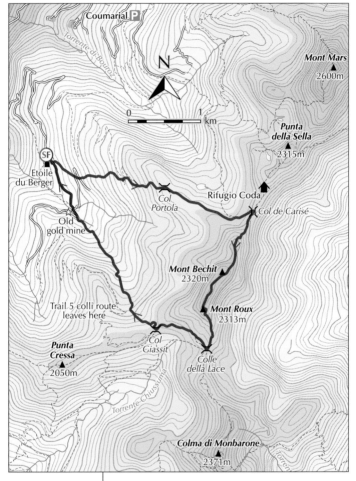

a directly uphill route. End of vehicle track, 1810m (**1hr 10min**).

Follow the path directly uphill to quickly gain height towards some well-kept buildings before trending right-ward to reach the Plan des Sorcières, a small plateau.

Route 4 – The Two Monts: Mont Roux and Mont Bechit

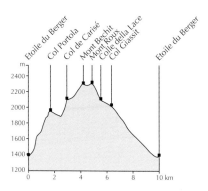

Follow the path upwards to arrive at the col and an impressive view that opens out, **Col Portola**, 1966m (**1hr 40min**).

Follow the path over the col into the basin and onwards to Col de Carisé. ▶

Follow the markings on the rock and climb to reach **Col de Carisé**, 2124m (**2hr 20min**).

The path never loses much height as it traverses across this basin. Keep an eye on the trail as it is rocky and it is easy to trip or slip on the worn rocks. The views serve as a substantial distraction!

Mont Bechit with Mont Roux behind; Colma di Mombarone in the distance

A sign for the GTA (Grande Traversata delle Alpi, a popular Italian long-distance trek that runs from the Swiss border to the Mediterranean, covering a total of 1000km) splits left.

A sign indicates Rifugio Coda to the left in 25 minutes. If a morning coffee does not appeal, take the route rightwards from the col and, in a few minutes, pass a second unnamed col at 2141m. ◄

Keep climbing steadily above a large cliff which buttresses the summit. Continue along the rightward trending path, which is well used as it is part of the Trail 5 Colli route as well as the AV1, following the obvious ridge line. Cross a number of false summits with small, steeper sections that are protected with fixed ropes and some footplates. Keep following the path as it skirts the summit dome to reach the actual summit of **Mont Bechit**, 2320m (**3hr 05min**). ◄

Keep an eye out for the mountain goats, which may be visible from the higher points, observing a walker's progress. Their curved horns might result in their misidentification as ibex but the bells around their necks are a giveaway.

Descending the fixed ropes with footplates to assist

Continue along the obvious summit ridge path as it undulates towards Mont Roux, 2313m (**3hr 20min**). ▸

A cross and a visitors' letter box adorn the summit; there are few English entries in the visitors' book. Follow the obvious descent path (which is steep) to start to arrive at **Colle della Lace**, 2117m (**3hr 40min**). ▸

The crossroads of paths at the col is a landmark for the area. Turn right and follow the well-worn path down to **Col Giassit**, 2026m (**4hr**).

From the col, descend to the right. The path is obvious to begin with but as it passes through higher pastures it can become indistinct. Be wary of following the Trail 5 Colli signs too far. At around 1850m the Trail 5 Colli breaks off left towards the dirt road visible on the hillside; this is NOT our route. As tempting as it may appear, it descends a completely different valley! Occasional yellow arrows are painted on the rocks and lead the way downwards. Follow an old aerial cableway and the yellow arrows towards the chalets of Larpit, 1637m. The path improves from here. Keep descending on the path on the left bank of the Torrent de Giassit to reach a minor road (**5hr**).

You can follow the road to the Etoile du Berger, but the gold mine, signposted over a small packhorse bridge, is worth a small detour. ▸ To return, follow the path wending its way along the field edges from the bridge or, alternatively, follow the road back to the **Etoile du Berger**, 1376m (**5hr 15min**).

There are spectacular views towards the Monte Rosa chain from here.

The map indicates a via ferrata here, but it is just some fixed ropes which can be used as handrails down the steeper sections. A few footplates help where there is a lack of obvious footholds and, before long, the gradient eases.

Beware of exploring too far into the open system; there is little health and safety advice beyond 'be careful'.

ROUTE 5
Colma di Mombarone

Start/Finish	Etoile du Berger, Sassa
Distance	11.5km
Ascent	965m
Descent	965m
Grade	2+ a very short section of fixed rope is nothing more than a handrail
Time	5hr 45min

An interesting but not too complex ridge offers basic scrambling to reach Punta Tre Vescovi and onwards to the pyramidal structure than sits on top of the summit of Colma di Mombarone, visible from quite a distance, which celebrates Christ the Redeemer.

A welcoming little mountain refuge, five minutes from the summit, offers enticing lunchtime options, and the view out from the Alps over the Piedmont region further adds to the special nature of the day.

For the best views an early start is recommended as the moisture-laden air from the plains tends to form clouds on the summits in the early afternoon.

For those wishing to complete this walk without staying at the Etoile du Berger, car parking is also possible close to the gold mine.

From the Etoile du Berger, 1376m, either descend to the path below the hotel and follow the path leftwards uphill or follow the road to end up at the abandoned gold mines **(10 min)**. ◄

Follow the road uphill for 100 metres until you reach a sharp hairpin bend and follow the sign for the AV1 (an inverted yellow triangle with 1 inside it), which follows the path above the river. As the path passes old farm buildings, it can become less obvious but always follows an uphill line.

At approximately 1680m the path meets a streambed about 100 metres after a stone barn. The arrows indicate continuing to the left of the streambed (right bank

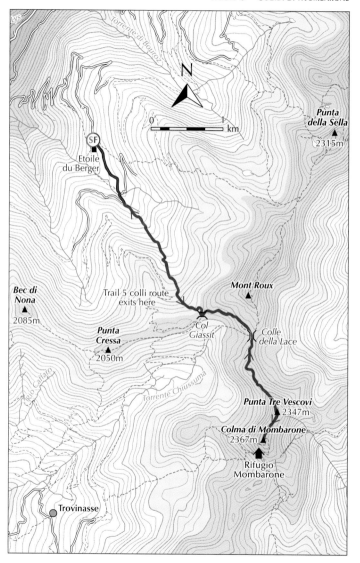

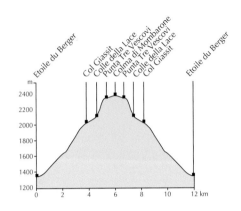

Overhead you will see a cable which is still used for transporting items to the summer farms on the higher reaches of the mountain.

in relation to streamflow), but if you cross the streambed a better route follows a worn path on this side of the stream, along the line of an old wall.

Reach the treeline at about 1750–1800m and pass more farm buildings. ◄ Cross the stream. The cross on Col Giassit is now visible high above. Follow the path taking a leftwards line to pass the highest farm buildings

The ridge and summit of Colma di Mombarone from Colle della Lace

and you will eventually reach **Col Giassit**, 2026m (**1hr 55min**). Mombarone will be visible to the right, with its distinctive summit monument. The next objective is Colle della Lace, which visible to the left.

Follow the obvious path to **Colle della Lace**, 2117m. ▶ (**2hr 20min**).

Follow the narrow path. After about 20 minutes some rocky steps are supported with metal fixed ropes. Use

A clear sign at the col is reassuring: 'Mombarone 2A, 1h 30mins'

Christ the Redeemer at the summit of Colma di Mombarone

Punta Tre Vescovi translates as the Peak of Three Bishops and marks the convergence of three dioceses, three communes (councils) and three provinces.

these cables to pass these challenges and continue following the path to reach the summit of **Punta Tre Vescovi**, 2347m (**3hr 25min**). ◀

The ridge from here is a simpler walk. Continue on the obvious path to reach **Colma di Mombarone**, 2367m (**3hr 45min**). The impressive tower at the summit of Colma di Mombarone was constructed in 1900 to celebrate Christ the Redeemer and offers superlative views. Two paths (red or yellow) lead down to the refuge and take about five minutes.

The return (which may well be in mist as the moisture-laden air rises and cools in the higher altitudes) is by the same path. At the summit of **Punta Tre Vescovi**, it is important to pay attention to route finding, as the path can be momentarily indistinct and two ridges lead off in northerly and easterly directions – the correct one is way-marked and bears to the left. Use the cables to pass the minor difficulties of the ridge in descent to return to **Colle della Lace**, 2117m (**4hr 40min**).

Turn left and retrace our morning route to return to **Col Giassit (5hr)**.

From here the return to Etoile du Berger is a little over an hour. ◀ Follow the occasional yellow arrows painted on the rocks towards the aerial cableway and onwards to reach the road close to the gold mine. Follow the road back to the starting point at **Etoile du Berger (5hr 45min)**.

Again, beware of following the Trail 5 Colli signs too far. At around 1850m the Trail 5 Colli route breaks off left towards the dirt road visible on the hillside. This is not the descent route to the Etoile du Berger.

The three diocese of Punta Tre Vescovi

70

ROUTE 6
Mont Mars traverse

Start/Finish	Parking at Coumarial, 1475m. Follow the road signposts for the Rifugio Barma from the main road between Fontainemore and Issime
Distance	Day 1: 5km; day 2: 7km
Ascent	Day 1: 680m; day 2: 720m
Descent	Day 1: 130m; day 2: 1270m
Grade	3
Time	Day 1: 2hr 45min; day 2: 6hr 35min

The summit of Mont Mars presides over the surrounding mountains and, as it is a difficult summit to reach, deserves to be named after the Roman god of war. You will certainly feel that a battle has been fought as you reach its lofty summit cross at 2600m, closer to the gods than mere mortals. Two options to reach the summit exist: one via a mountain path, the other via the Ciao Miki via ferrata (they join at Col Cappi shortly before the final summit slopes). A long and challenging descent, making use of fixed ropes, followed by a descent across a boulder field makes this a full mountain day. All but the ultra-fit will stay overnight at Rifugio Barma, possibly the most luxurious mountain hut in existence.

It is important to book into the refuge and to have checked the weather forecast. Moisture-laden air rising from the Piedmont plain causes a lot of cloud formation in the afternoons, which makes navigation on the descent more difficult as spotting the painted markers on the boulder field can be challenging.

Day 1
From the parking follow signs for the refuge along a continuation of the road which is closed except for access from this point; stone steps shortcut the road's zigzags. Follow the road to a signpost at a little wooden bridge (**5min**).

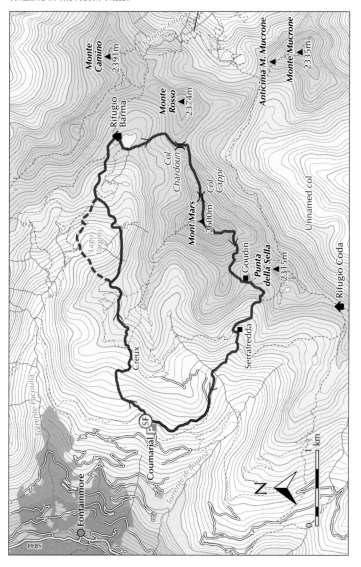

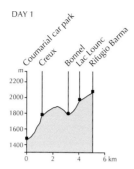

DAY 1

Take this path (also identifying Path 2D to Mont Mars) and follow it into woodland. Climb through the forest to reach a path junction (not indicated on the map), 1685m (**30min**).

Take the path to the right. ▶ Continue climbing to reach the chalet of **Creux**, 1788m (**45min**).

Cross the track and continue following the path (signposted for the refuge and Path 2D) upwards to join the well-worn trail of the AV1, 1868m (**55min**).

Turn left and follow the AV1, passing a shed to join a track which soon becomes a path. Pass a small pond and begin to descend to reach a pyramidal signpost marker, 1880m (**1hr 15min**).

Two options exist here: the first is to follow the AV1 and drop to the dam of **Lago Vargno** before climbing to the refuge. This will take approximately an hour and a half. The other is to take the newly numbered Path 2C (unnumbered but marked on the map) which traverses the hillside above the lake. This is a rougher path and has short sections of fixed rope. However, it also serves as a good testing ground in preparation for tomorrow (if you find this path uncomfortably difficult, then Mont Mars is not for you).

Path 2C enters the forest and within 15 minutes you will encounter a few fixed-rope sections before reaching a bridge (**1hr 45min**).

Shortly after this junction there is a reassuring sign for the Trail 5 Colli.

73

Rifugio Barma approach path, day 1

After a short climb to the chalets of Bonnel, follow the path sharp right and traverse across to meet the AV1 shortly before the cow sheds of Lac Lounc, 1945m (**2hr 10min**).

For those attempting this in a single day, take Path 2B directly to Col Chardoun. Otherwise, follow the AV1 to climb to the left of the large rock bastion ahead. From here the refuge is in sight, about 10 minutes away. Follow the path to **Rifugio Barma**, 2047m (**2hr 45min**).

> The **refuge** is in a beautiful setting close to the lake, and a lazy couple of hours can be enjoyed relaxing by the lakeside or on the balcony of the refuge with a coffee and a slice of home-made cake.
>
> Rifugio Barma (independent, sleeps 54, tel +39 331 1087009, rifugiobarma@gmail.com www.rifugio barma.it).

Day 2
An early start is a good idea – it should allow a summit time free of any cloud.

Begin by locating the path which skirts the lake and passes below the small hut visible from the refuge. Cross a stream to join Path 2B, passing the old huts of Barmetta (**20min**).

Keep a close eye on the markings as an unmarked path leads leftwards into a gully. The correct path trends further right and is waymarked 2B. Continue on this path to reach the **Col Chardoun**, 2221m (**45min**).

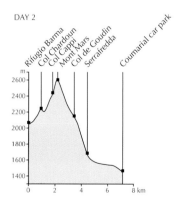

A chairlift from Biella allows access from that valley so it tends to be busier here.

From the col descend a short distance and take the path rightwards, traversing beneath the ridgeline. ◄

This path steadily climbs to the side of the ridgeline which is the via ferrata. On occasions the two routes meet, but the path is well used and keeps off the summit line. As such, a mixed party can enjoy this day with experienced via ferrata-ists taking the ridge and walkers following the path.

After approximately an hour the path and via ferrata join at **Col Cappi**, 2440m (**1hr 45min**).

The view is very impressive: a sea of clouds cover the Piedmont plain below, the pyramidal structure on Colma di Mombarone is clearly visible beyond the 'Two Monts' of Roux and Bechit and the higher summits of Monte Rosa and Gran Paradiso can also be made out.

From the col, the summit of Mont Mars is a rough path that splits and rejoins as it clambers up the slopes above. A couple of short sections are quite strenuous and involve fixed ropes to assist balance. After around 50 minutes you will finally reach the summit of **Mont Mars**, 2600m (**2hr 35min**). ◄

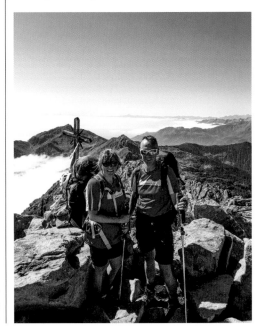

A well-earned break on the summit of Mont Mars

Traversing the fixed ropes on the decent route

It is possible to return to Rifugio Barma from here by retracing your steps. This is likely to take about two hours. However, for the full mountain experience continue the traverse.

From the summit cross follow the markers for Rifugio Coda. The path begins easily and height is lost quite quickly. Zigzag down the slopes, following the worn path and occasional marker, to the first fixed ropes, 2550m (**3hr 05min**).

These ropes traverse the mountainside in the sun before a short climb to an unnamed col, 2546m (**3hr 30min**).

The ropes are now on the north-facing side of the mountain and in the shade. Small pockets of snow can linger here, so be sure of foot placements on this side of the mountain. There are short unroped sections on the easier ground – concentration is essential. Within 10 minutes the ropes once again return on the sunny side of the ridge. (**3hr 40min**)

Descend to reach a rocky point and a steep descent to Col de Goudin, 2428m (**4hr 10min**).

The route drops to the right here, signed for Rifugio Coda. It seems impossible from the approach but fixed ropes pick a line down to a path junction (**4hr 25min**).

At this junction take the right-hand option, Path 3A. The waymarking is yellow spots, arrows or circles with 3A written on them. Keep a careful eye out for the way-markings across the boulder field.

After around 15 minutes the Col de Goudin becomes visible on the right and a path below it traverses the hill-side. After crossing the boulders, follow the path down to the abandoned chalets of **Goudin**, 2103m (**5hr 15min**).

From here cross the stream to join the AV1 and follow this to reach the chalet of **Serrafredda**, 1841m (**5hr 40min**).

Be careful not to continue on the AV1 at this point. Take the path that drops to the left of the chalet, still the 3A, passing (but not crossing) a bridge after five minutes where Path 3 joins. Continue descending on the 3A to a well-built wooden bridge (**6hr**).

Cross this bridge and follow the path to join a track at Vercosa, 1560m (**6hr 10min**). While the map indicates the 3A wends its way across the hillside, in fact we follow the track to eventually reach the road above **Coumarial** (**6hr 30min**).

Turn left and follow the road back to the car park, 1475m (**6hr 35min**).

UPPER LYS VALLEY

Looking down into the Lys valley from the Belvedere (Route 8)

The upper Lys valley is a hidden beauty; the villages of Gressoney-Saint-Jean, Gressoney-La-Trinité and Staffal, at the head of the valley, appear almost timeless. The quiet streets are overshadowed by steep valley sides and the Lys flows relentlessly down the valley. Another settlement of note is Alpenzu, 350m above the valley bottom and about halfway between the two Gressoneys. This hamlet is clearly visible from Gressoney-Saint-Jean and commands a breathtaking view.

The unique culture and architecture of the upper valley stem from the Walser influence. The distinctive building style, with a strongly overhanging upper balcony and wooden walls, owes its origin to the people from the Valais region in Switzerland who travelled and settled here in the 13th and 14th centuries. Subsequent glacial advance closed the passes they used as communication routes, thereby creating a pocket of Swiss culture and an architectural style that survives to the present day. The German–Swiss feel to the valley is most obvious in the linguistic roots of the Walser dialect, which means many places have two spelling variations of their names.

The other defining influence on the valley was Queen Margherita. Her love of the mountains and its people made the valley a 'must do' for those seeking her favour and attention. A number of large houses around Gressoney-Saint-Jean were built by those seeking the queen's favour and attention. Her own home, built at the turn of the 20th century, is Castel Savoia; a pleasant 40-minute walk from Gressoney-Saint-Jean, the castle is now open to the public. More well known to those of a mountaineering background is the highest refuge in the Alps: Rifugio Margherita on Punta Gnifetti (4554m). In 1893 the queen visited the refuge. The ascent is still a significant climb, even with modern cable cars and equipment; without these aids it would have been a formidable challenge indeed.

At the head of the valley is the bulk of the enormous Monta Rosa massif. The massif comprises a huge plain of ice with a substantial number of peaks exceeding 4000m reaching out of the ice field, including the second highest mountain in the Alps, the Dufourspitze (4634m).

A regular *navette* (shuttle bus) runs in the upper valley, which can make travelling easier and allows walkers to take linear routes should they wish to do so.

There is no shortage of accommodation in the upper valley; it is a popular ski area and, in summer, there are plenty of self-catering apartments and hotel rooms available. Camping in the valley is more limited than might be expected. A basic site at Gressoney-Saint-Jean is the only option and offers camping and camper van accommodation. It also has some rooms with shared catering and bathroom facilities, although these are above the games room and are unlikely to be tranquil in the school holiday season.

The ski lift system is open during the summer, which significantly reduces ascent times and allows walkers to gain height and enjoy views of the high mountains.

Gressoney-Saint-Jean is the largest centre; it offers a range of cafés and restaurants, a few small supermarkets and local produce stores, as well as medical facilities, a pharmacy and a bank with a cash dispenser. Some small outdoor shops sell essentials, and maps and guidebooks can also be bought in the centre of the village.

Map: 1:25,000 Carta dei Sentieri by L'Escursionista Editore 8: Monte Rosa – Alte Valli d'Ayas e de Lys.

ROUTE 7
Via Regina to Castel Savoia

Start/Finish	Gressoney-Saint-Jean
Distance	3.5km
Ascent	40m
Descent	40m
Grade	1
Time	1hr 20min

A gentle ramble along a popular path arrives at the Castel Savoia, Queen Margherita's alpine hideaway. With limited height gain and a good track, this walk will appeal to the rambler in search of a morning's stroll or to a whole family looking for a mini adventure.

The castle was used by the royal family each summer as their principal holiday home and gives an insight into life a hundred years ago. The alpine garden will also be of interest to the keen botanist and is free to explore.

It is worth confirming the opening hours of the Castel Savoia to make the most of your visit. Be aware that tours are only available as a guided group and may not always be available in English, although an English pamphlet is available.

From the upper square in Gressoney-Saint-Jean (the one with the Arthemisia Cibo E Vino delicatessen and snack bar café slightly uphill of the church), take the cobbled road westwards, passing the shops and Pizzeria Oro Argento Bronzo (Gold, Silver and Bronze). ▶ The path is the AV1 (marked with a 1 inside a triangle). The rough road quickly becomes a footpath leading past some fields. Take a sharp left turn on the path and pass above the popular lakes to climb slightly and reach a path junction with Path 4A. Follow the AV1 path onwards, signed 'Castello Savoia, 20min' (**20min**).

This pizzeria is owned by Olympic and World Championship Nordic skier Arianna Follis. Her medals and trophies are on display in the restaurant. Great pizzas too!

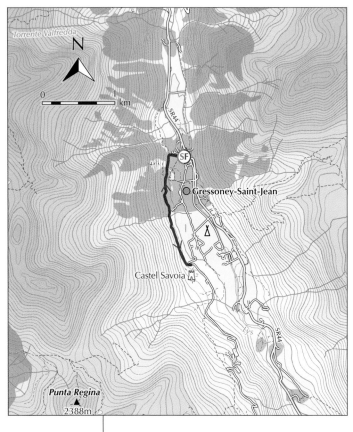

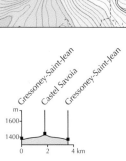

After crossing a **bridge**, climb slightly before dropping to **Castel Savoia**. Follow this obvious path with care as it opens into the visitors' car park (**40min**).

Castel Savoia

The return is the same path in reverse, which takes a similar time.

ROUTE 8

Punta Regina:
the queen's peak

Start/Finish	Weissmatten chairlift car park, south of Gressoney-Saint-Jean
Distance	6km
Ascent	505m
Descent	505m
Grade	2
Time	3hr 20min

No visit to Gressoney-Saint-Jean would be complete without discovering the legacy of Queen Margherita; this is reputed to have been one of her favourite walks and the views are certainly fit for a queen!

This is a short walk but it includes a reasonable amount of ascent and some rougher paths so it is graded 2. It would make a perfect first peak, and the extensive views throughout the day range from Mont Blanc to Gran Paradiso and the Monte Rosa massif. The spectacular eyrie of the Belvedere offers an impressive viewpoint of the upper Lys valley. A day for views indeed, so don't forget a camera!

The Weissmatten chairlift reduces the ascent and allows for a relaxed view of the mountains. It is perfectly possible to reach the chairlift base station via the 'Queen's Way' and a short section of the AV1 from Castel Savoia.

Another interesting discovery is the small shrine that marks the crossing from one valley to another, while a plaque commemorates Tolstoy's passage in 1857; this route is certainly a walk into history.

It is worth checking the last lift times and any possible midday closures before departing the top lift station.	The day begins with an uplift on the chairlift of the World Cup ski run to **Weissmatten**, 2043m. ◀
	The path departs from the top lift station between trees to the right of the reservoir (not marked on the 1:25,000 map) and behind a lovely old wooden chalet, privately owned. A sign indicates the way, Path 3A.

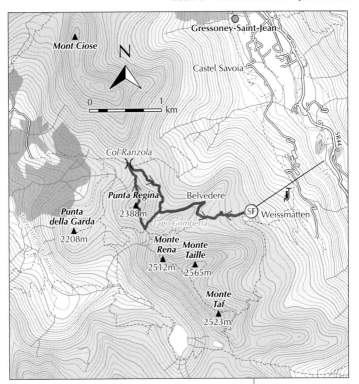

Having located the correct path, follow it as it steadily gains height. Given the relatively high starting point the ascent will make the unacclimatised walker feel it is harder than expected. A slow and steady pace is recommended, which will also allow time to observe the variety of **plants and flowers**, including the larch, pine and mountain ash forest as well as alpenrose, which flowers until late July.

At the first waypoint of the day, a small stone chalet at 2160m, Alpe Prato (marked on the map as Wissomatto), take the obvious path to the right and continue to climb

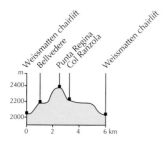

more open slopes with wild blueberries, ripening by late July, to reach **Belvedere**, 2210m **(45min)**.

The **viewpoint** here is stunning. The valley seems so far below and the backdrop of Monte Rosa complements the scene perfectly. It is important to be aware of the substantial drop in front of the viewpoint; children should be kept close by!

Punta Regina's rounded summit is visible through the trees.

Continue in a westerly direction along the path. After a couple of hundred metres there are some fixed ropes to aid the descent of a rougher section. ◀ The path leaves the trees in favour of an open, fairly level section. Follow the path as it picks its way across the stony ground to reach an open basin which has the remains of **Lago Gombetta (1hr)**. In high summer this will be little more

Enjoying the approach to Lago Gombetta

86

The view from the summit of Punta Regina

than a puddle but serves as a crossroads of paths. Punta Regina is clearly visible and doesn't seem too far.

Follow Path 3A to the left towards the pass, a dip in the skyline, Passo della Garda. ▶

Before reaching the pass take Path 3A to the right to reach the rounded summit of **Punta Regina**, 2388m (**1hr 45min**).

Surprisingly, for such a regal sounding mountain there is no significant **summit structure**. A cross would be expected but instead the view must act as the celebration – and what a view! On a clear day the bulk of Mont Blanc is visible ahead. The highest mountain entirely situated within Italy, Gran Paradiso, can also be seen.

While traversing the hillside you will see a memorial, below on the right, to Leonardo Follis, a local skier and brother of Arianna, who tragically died in an avalanche in 2001.

*Santa Maria,
Col Ranzola*

Leave the summit along the same path as the ascent but be attentive to the descent path (7A) which splits to the left within about 40 metres. The descent path is not too clearly marked from the summit area and care needs to be taken to avoid following the previously used ascent path rightwards too far.

The descent is steep to begin with and twists as it descends towards the bulk of Monte Ciosè and, more importantly, a chapel and col visible below.

The path splits significantly at one point but neither option is particularly right or wrong; they both meet again before too long.

At approximately 2240m there is a level section of hillside, almost a ridge line. The path splits into several smaller paths here; the furthest left may seem to be the best option but loses its presence quite quickly with a dead end, so stay further right.

At the drystone wall, an unusual feature in the Alps, the path improves. Follow the path to reach **Col Ranzola**, 2171m (**2hr 15min**).

> The **wall** marks the boundary of the two valleys and leads down to the chapel and col below. This was once a major travelling route, as traders passed from the Piedmont plain to descend to the Ayas valley and continue onwards to the Valais in Switzerland. A small plaque commemorates the crossing in 1857 of probably the most famous traveller along this route, Leo Tolstoy.
>
> The **small chapel**, common in the Alps, allowed travellers to give thanks or request the help of a significant saint. This one is dedicated to Santa Maria. Cols are often the crossroads of paths and this is no exception.

Several paths go their separate ways from here and sourcing the correct one is important. The return path to Lago Gombetta is 3B. It is the most level of those available but may be overlooked in favour of the more worn 3 or 3C. The signpost indicates that the top of the chairlift is approximately one hour away.

Follow the delightful, gently descending Path 3B across the open hillside and round the shoulder to return to the **small lake at Gombetta**, 2186m, to rejoin Path 3A from earlier (**2hr 35min**).

Cross the open, rocky slope on the path, the fixed ropes are more useful in ascent than they may have been when descending, to reach the Belvedere once more. Keep on Path 3A to arrive back at the **Weissmatten chairlift** (**3hr 20min**). ▸

A small restaurant close to the lake offers a fine view and refreshments before you return by lift to the valley below.

ROUTE 9

Alpenzu and the Walser villages

Start/Finish	Gressoney-Saint-Jean parking (payable) is plentiful near the road bridge over the River Lys
Distance	12.5km
Ascent	540m
Descent	540m
Grade	2
Time	4hr 10min

A lovely walk along part of the Grande Sentiero Walser above the upper valley gives you time to explore and understand the folk life of times gone by. The Walser people and their culture originated from the Swiss canton of Valais, and their influence remains a feature of the upper Lys valley today.

The route passes through numerous Walser settlements, including the high hamlet of Alpenzu, which stares down from its lofty perch above the upper valley. After a sharp climb the route undulates along the valley sides through pleasant meadows and woodland.

It is also feasible to complete the second half of the route, from Gressoney-La-Trinité back to Gressoney-Saint-Jean, using the valley bus to reach the starting point. This would be a gentle walk of a couple of hours.

THE WALSER CULTURE

The Walser people and their associated cultural identity once spread across the Alps; today small pockets remain in remote corners, and two such areas can be found in the upper Lys valley. Before the mini ice age, which saw rapid glacial advances in the 1300s, people travelled from the Valais to the upper valleys of the Aya and Lys. The passes were clear in the summer so trade and travel were problem free. Within a generation, glacial advances closed off the passes and the people of the Valais who had crossed the mountains found themselves unable to return home. Across the Alps legends

Traditional Walser chalets

tell of witches and curses causing a hundred years of winter, while scientists identify this as the beginning of the mini ice age.

The distinctive Walser chalet style can be observed in the upper Lys region. The buildings are on stone stilts and have balconies with overhanging upper floors; the balconies often have full-width wooden bars. The Walser people maintained their own cultural identity, including traditional dress and language, which bears more than a resemblance to German. Although the dialect has died out to some extent, there is a strong desire to keep the language alive.

The Grande Sentiero Walser (GSW) is a long-distance trek reflecting the journeys made by the Walser people long ago. It begins at Issime in the lower Lys valley and ascends the Lys valley before crossing Colle Pinter to the head of the Ayas valley. It then continues on over the Col Nord des Cimes Blanches and on to Colle del Teodulo beneath the Matterhorn. It takes around five days to complete.

From the car park take the AV1 signed path, cross the wooden bridge and follow the river's left bank. Pass the **golf course** to a road bridge (**25min**).

Take this bridge to cross the river to **Tschemenoal** (Chemonal) and turn right to follow the road for about 200 metres. The path to Alpenzu (Path 6) leaves the road

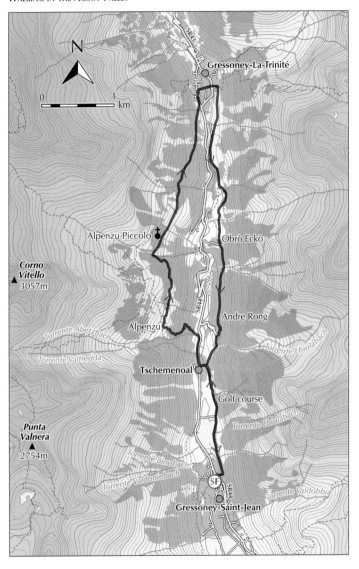

shortly after the stream crosses the road. Take this path through the mixed forest to reach the hamlet of **Alpenzu**, 1770m **(1hr 30min)**.

As the path wends its way through the 13 houses that make up the hamlet

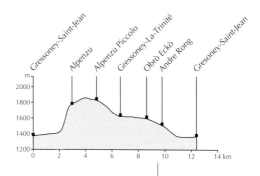

(which dates back to the 1200s), make sure you locate Path 1W, the Walserweg to Alpenzu Piccolo. A large rock marks the path divergence, Path 1W to the right. A few minutes later the path splits again; take the left fork. A

Alpenzu sitting high above the valley

93

painted sign shortly after this fork is reassuring. Pass some old farm buildings as the path rises and falls along the hillside.

Take time to enjoy the views back towards Gressoney-Saint-Jean along this section.

After an undulating wander, there's no rush, you will arrive at a path junction (**1hr 55min**). ◄

Take the path uphill and leftwards, (the GSW path) which again indicates Alpenzu Piccolo. Climb uphill for around five minutes to another junction and signpost. Follow the GSW sign and, in a couple of hundred metres,

The views open out here through breaks in the forest.

cross a wooden bridge and a high point of 1855m. ◄ Pass the junction with Path 7A and enter **Alpenzu Piccolo**, 1807m, a great place for a rest (no facilities) (**2hr 20min**).

Pass the lovely little church and continue to descend. Cross a stream over an impressive piece of stonework and

Take care as the path steepens its descent.

pass a small shrine and memorial. ◄ The path meets Path 10A. Enter the forest (following Path 1W signs) for a short while. (Note: this path is not marked on the 1:25,000

The picturesque townhall in Gressoney-La-Trinité

map.) After crossing a large floodwater channel you will arrive at the village of **Gressoney-La-Trinité**, 1635m (**2hr 45min**). ▶

This is a small village with limited facilities.

Follow signs to pass by the tourist office and exit the small square 'top left' to cross the bridge over the river to the main valley road and signs indicating 'GSW Gressoney-Saint-Jean' (**2hr 50min**).

The return path is Path 15 (although this is marked as Path 14 on the 1:25,000 map). After 100 metres take the path as it leaves the track between buildings (signs are clearly painted on the wall here); this path joins a dirt road. Pass a stone works and as the path bends right continue straight on (yellow marker stone on the ground). After a wooden bridge a signpost confirms the path (Path 15). Pass a pylon on a farm track and bear right on the narrow path (**3hr 05min**).

Follow the obvious dirt track towards the hamlet of **Obrò Eckò** (which means 'upper corner' in the Walser dialect). Keep an eye out for a yellow arrow indicating the path to the hamlet. This path is lovely, wending its way through some impressive buildings, including an archway and small chapel. Follow the narrow path as it rises to rejoin the track and follow it through the next hamlet of Obro Biela. Here bear left onto what appears to be a private, cobbled driveway and a reassuring signpost (**3hr 30min**).

Follow the path along the side of the stone wall to arrive at **Andre Rong**, Walser for 'the other dead end' – not too inspiring for a walk! This collection of ancient Walser buildings is enchanting and worthy of admiration. Follow the path to meet a road at Rong, about 500 metres further on. Locate and follow the path which drops between the houses and skirts Villa Loubeno to rejoin the road. (It is possible to stay on the road to avoid the drop and climb of the path here) (**3hr 50min**). ▶

These mansion houses were popular with those wishing to gain favour with the royal family, hence the number of large houses seen in the Gressoney area, following Queen Margherita's patronage of the area.

Take the path as it drops from the road on a more direct line to meet the pleasant, wide track that follows the river through the golf course back to Gressoney-Saint-Jean (**4hr 10min**).

ROUTE 10
Source of the Lys

Start/Finish	Staffal car park
Distance	6km
Ascent	600m
Descent	600m
Grade	2
Time	3hr

Where a glacier gives birth to a river, a fascinating geographical journey begins. These places are very special. Standing at the edge of the living world and staring upwards across the icy, lifeless landscape gives the walker time to reflect and ponder. Glacial retreat means that this walk has significantly more height gain than some local leaflets might suggest; the source of the river is creeping up the mountainside as the glacier retreats. Nevertheless, this is a walk into another world and a unique experience.

A small supermarket is passed on the right-hand side and may be useful for any last-minute supplies.

The path leaves the road at a sharp left turn above the car park towards the head of the valley (top right of the car park looking up the valley). Follow the path along the left bank of the river which is clearly signed as Path 7. ◄

Follow the path to enter the trees, passing through the predominantly larch forest and then by some farm buildings to reach the upper treeline and a path junction, 2165m (**50min**).

The open meadows will be strewn with **wildflowers** in high summer and it is worth taking a moment to enjoy the views into the valley below and beyond. Along the side of the path you will see mountain houseleek looking like a small pink anemone. Harebells and campion will add a splash of blue, while alpine daisies and aster will reflect the sunny

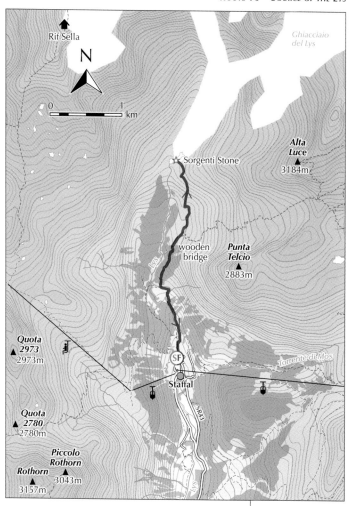

yellow of a perfect Alpine day. Early in the season alpenrose (wild roses) will also be found among the trees and on the open ground.

The indication of 35 minutes is reasonably accurate for an acclimatised walker but may be optimistic if this is a first walk or you're a mixed family group.

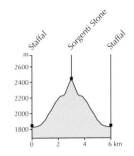

When you consider how much ice filled this little valley less than 20 years ago you are reminded of how quickly the glaciers are receding.

Take the path signed to the Sorgenti del Lys, Path 7. ◄

After a short descent, cross a **wooden bridge** and begin climbing the old glacial lateral moraine; as recently as 2002 this was the extent of the glacier.

From the crest of the moraine the ice-smoothed rock in the glacial basin is clearly visible as is the moraine on what was the opposite side of the glacier. ◄

Keep climbing (quite steeply for a short while) and soon it will be possible to see other people at the **Sorgenti Stone** 2417m (**1hr 45min**).

Climbing out of Staffal

Monte Rosa from the Sorgenti Stone

The view from the *sorgenti* (source) stone makes the climb worthwhile in itself. The vast ice fields of the Monte Rosa chain seem almost close enough to touch; the glacial tongues reach down while the Lys valley leads to the south. ▶

For those interested in getting up close to the glacial landscape, some indistinct paths wend their way towards the glacial meltwater lake, a constantly changing environment so barren of life as to appear to be lunar. The lake is constantly changing as the glacier retreats; the shoreline is unstable and the water will be very cold indeed.

To return to Staffal retrace the ascent route which will take around 1 hour and 15 minutes (**3hr**).

With the aid of some binoculars it may be possible to spot alpinists on the mountains above. There are unlikely to be many better places to enjoy a picnic lunch!

Note: some older maps and route descriptions indicate that the Sorgenti Stone is at 2161m; this was the old position until the rapid, recent retreat of the glacier to 2417m. No doubt future retreat will only increase the ascent to the new source of the Lys.

ROUTE 11
Punta Indren and Indren glacier crossing

Start	Staffal; Passo dei Salati (lift station), 2940m
Finish	Punta Indren lift station, 3280m
Distance	2.5km
Ascent	420m
Descent	70m (if returning on the lift)
Grade	3+ or Alpine Mountaineering: F
Time	1hr 45min (allow 30 minutes for the uplift and an hour for the descent)

With ski lifts operating throughout the summer months, it is perfectly possible to enjoy a high mountain ridge, cross the foot of a glacier and feel like you're in the thrones of the mountain gods.

Although this is not a technical route, it requires a range of elementary mountaineering skills, steady footwork and a head for heights. There is protection in the form of fixed ropes where needed, but a walker on this route will need experience of steep ground. The route crosses permanent snow fields and, technically, a glacier, although this is little more than another very gently angled snow field with an icy base. Sturdy boots, a trekking pole or two and warmer clothing than that worn for lower walks should suffice in the summer.

For those with an interest in glaciology the recently exposed rocks, previously covered by ice for hundreds of years, will be of great interest. The striation lines, formed when small pebbles become trapped within the ice and scrape along the bedrock, are worth keeping an eye out for while approaching the top lift station at Punta Indren.

The lifts from Staffal are quick and quite reasonably priced: €20 return in 2020. It is worth noting the lift times for the day before setting off.

The route begins at the top lift station, Passo dei Salati, 2940m. The colder air will come as quite a shock when leaving the protective bubble of the lift which started in much warmer climes. ◄

From the lift station Path 6C begins at the far end of the low building. Begin by ascending the steep, wide track which climbs above the building before breaking

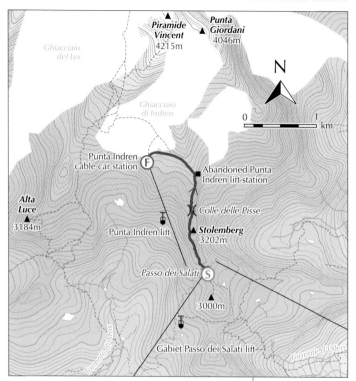

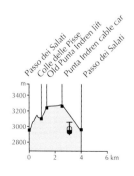

off left. ▶ Climb steadily on the path, passing rare alpine flowers not seen in the lower valley, including edelweiss, alpine toad flax, moss campion, alpine mouse-ear and spring gentians, to reach the base of the ridge and some fixed ropes (**15min**).

Signage only consists of occasionally marked stones and cairns but the path is evident enough on the ground.

101

The fixed ropes leading to Colle delle Pisse

Ibex might well be encountered along the ridge; they prefer the high, lonely mountainsides.

Bear to the right of the ridge to the fixed ropes traversing the mountainside before returning to the left-hand side of the ridge. The ground becomes more and more rocky and broken but stay on the obvious line through the cold-shattered boulders to pass beneath the summit of Stolemberg (**30min**). ◀

The abandoned cable car station of Punta Indren is visible on the ridge ahead. The modern one is far off to the left.

Ahead appears an impossibly steep descent but this proves to be a lot simpler than it might first appear. Fixed ropes assist through the more challenging sections. ◀

Descend towards the col, Col delle Pisse. This is a serious mountain environment; care needs to be taken not to dislodge any loose rock. A couple of steeper descents may be best approached by downclimbing using the ropes to assist you. There is nothing more challenging here than, say, Crib Goch.

Arrive at **Colle delle Pisse**, 3110m, where you are likely to encounter the first snow patch on the right of the ridge **(55min)**.

The view towards the Monte Rosa chain is worth admiring before tackling the final ascent to the abandoned station, **Punta Indren**, 3260m **(1hr 15min)**.

The new cable car station has an indistinct path leading to it, Path 6C (this path does not follow the line marked on the map at present). Follow the path with occasional cairns to aid route finding. Snow will cover some parts of the route but there is usually a trodden path to follow and the snow patches are only for a short distance. Continue towards the obvious bulk of the cable car station and cross a final, larger snow field before the snout of the glacier is reached. ▶ Follow the edge of the glacier to the left and down to the wide tracks that lead to the **Punta Indren cable car station (1hr 45min)**.

This is usually quite a busy place as it is the starting point for some of the Monte Rosa summits and is also a popular starting point for glacier walks with local guides.

Exploring the higher reaches of the glaciers with a guide is a popular summer trip

The **cable car station** was an island of rock surrounded by the glacier until less than 10 years ago. Today, there is a lot of evidence of glacial erosion. Striations on the bedrock are clearly visible: scratches made on the bedrock by small rocks embedded within the glacier as it moved over the mountain base. Lateral moraines (large, steep ridges of rubble) are deposited by the slower moving edge of the glacier and indicate its previous height and width. Meltwater lakes are dotted around the landscape and are subject to continual formation as the glacier retreats. The rubble that sits on top of the glacial sheet forms terminal moraines at the front (snout) of the glacier and often forms dams for meltwater lakes.

There are no facilities at this station during the summer months; two options are now possible. The first is to return by the ascent path; this will take a similar amount of time and will allow features noticed on the route out to be explored in more depth. The second is to descend by cable car to the Passo dei Salati. At the time of writing, there did not appear to be a system that allowed you to pay for a single descent and, in the author's experience, the lift operators aren't too concerned that the ticket purchased for the return trip to Passo di Salati doesn't work; everyone is accommodated on the lift, but there is no guarantee that entry will be allowed without a valid ticket! Also be aware that this lift runs infrequently and is likely to be the first to be cancelled in the likelihood of bad weather.

ROUTE 12

Bettolina ridge to Rifugio Quintino Sella

Start/Finish	Passo di Bettaforca, 2672m lift station
Distance	8km
Ascent	980m
Descent	980m
Grade	3 or Alpine Mountaineering: F
Time	5hr 30min

Fixed ropes and metal work in the upper reaches of this route might indicate it takes the form of a via ferrata; it is probably reasonable to call this a protected walk as no-one seems to have via ferrata equipment on the route.

Starting pretty much at the limit of the vegetation, this walk has the feel of a serious mountain day. The route is well marked and easy to follow but that doesn't mean it is easy. Local signs rate it as 'EE' but due to the high altitude and a couple of exposed sections it may also be worthy of a 'Facile' Alpine grading.

Having said all that, it is a popular excursion as the lift system allows the route to begin at 2700m, leaving approximately 1000m to reach the Rifugio Quintino Sella 3585m, which is set in a spectacular position and offers hot meals and refreshments in a stunning setting. The Glacier di Felik curves past the back of the refuge barely 20 metres away and the backdrop of the Monte Rosa chain is truly magical.

The lifts from Staffal are a two-stage affair: the first is a 450m ascent, while the chairlift saves another 500m ascent. ▶

From the Bettaforca chairlift station, take the path (or follow the vehicle track) to the right of the buildings; they both meet after 200 metres. The sign to the refuge points in the right general direction. Although waymarking for Path 9 is initially limited, once clear of the ski station

This return journey will cost around €20 (2020). It is important to be aware of the final departure times of the upper lift before departing in the morning.

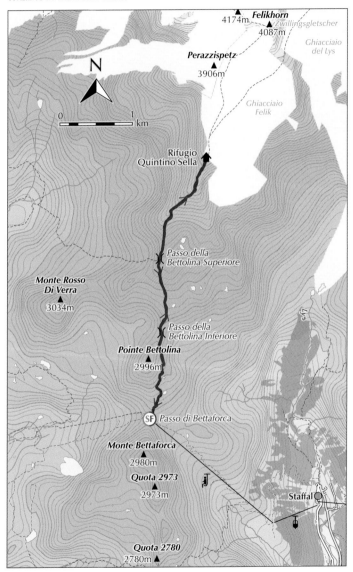

clutter it becomes easier to identify as the route settles into a more
usual mountain path.

By the time you encounter
the first small lake, (**15min**), the
path and route will be clear.

Keep on the path to reach
the col of **Passo della Bettolina
Inferiore**, 2905m (**45min**).

Keep following the path
along the ridge, which becomes
narrow in places, to reach the
col of **Passo della Bettolina
Superiore**, 3100m (**1hr 10min**).

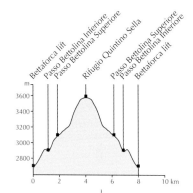

*The rope certainly
helps on the
steeper sections*

The route now takes on a more mountainous feel. Keep an eye out for the painted waymarking as the route climbs among the boulder fields. Keep following the Path 9 marks and yellow spots on rocks; cairns and standing stones are also helpful markers. You will encounter the first metalwork at approximately 3200m. Climb the small outcrop (only a few metres in height) to gain its top (**2hr**). ◄

If you find this little outcrop intimidating then it may be better to turn back here.

Continue climbing the rocky slope. The ground is generally stable but always be on your guard for unstable rocks. You will reach a large cairn at 3353m (**2hr 20min**).

A short level section follows. Snow patches may be encountered here but they are reasonably level and straightforward to cross.

After crossing this section, you will reach the final fixed-rope section (**2hr 30min**). ◄

Trekking poles are best stored on packs before beginning these roped sections of the route.

Begin by following the simple rope handrail along the shattered rock ridge. After this horizontal handrail section, a double-roped ascent follows, one rope for each hand; this is only a few metres in height. Follow the ropes along the exposed ridgeline to reach a wooden bridge over a significant gap in the ridgeline (**2hr 40min**).

Continue following the rope as it wends its way along a narrow path. Climb via steps and fixed metalwork to reach a level ridge on which the refuge is built (**2hr 55min**).

A short walk follows to reach the door of the **Rifugio Quintino Sella**, 3585m (**3hr**).

The **refuge** is situated on a safe plateau, protected from likely avalanche dangers, and is close to the glacier. It uses glacial water and all supplies are flown in by helicopter. Food and refreshments are available and a hearty menu is on offer.

The descent is by the same route. Care needs to be taken as descending can present different but significant challenges. Additionally, during the afternoon the path will be used by alpinists climbing up to the refuge for the night, ready to ascend the nearby peaks in the morning. This will mean a degree of 'giving way'. All in all, the descent will probably take around 2hr 30min, as the upper section demands care and time to descend safely. The marking seems to be more obvious in descent than ascent and the popularity of the path means a number of other users will probably act as mobile waymarkers! (**5hr 30min**).

RIFUGIO QUINTINO SELLA AL FELIK

A warm welcome in a cold place, the Rifugio Quintino Sella

There has been a mountain hut on this shoulder since 1885 when two local CAI chapters combined efforts to build a permanent refuge. It is named after Senator Quintino Sella, founder of the CAI, who had died the year before in the local town of Biella.

The first wooden structure could host 15 people and materials were carried by the workers to the site!

Within 20 years the weather had worn the building so much a replacement was required which was built slightly higher up the mountain. In 1910 the Roveyaz family became guardians and continued as such for 60 years.

Following World War 2 the hut was dismantled to avoid potential avalanche risk and was rebuilt on its current site.

Communication was improved in the 1970s with the installation of a radio telephone, and the chairlift construction at Colle Bettaforca in 1977 made access significantly easier.

The current refuge was opened in 1981 and can host 142 people. With the famous Castor and Pollux nearby, the hut is a very popular starting point for an ascent of these 4000m summits.

THE MONTE ROSA CHAIN

The eastern edge of the Monte Rosa massif

The mountain range that forms the backdrop to the Lys and Ayas valleys is the enormous Monte Rosa group, the largest chain in the Alps. Beginning with the Breithorn in the west and continuing to Punta Gnifetti in the east, it includes the second highest summit in the Alps, Dufourspitze at 4634m, on the Swiss side of the chain.

Many will think the name refers to the pink tinge seen at a typical summer sunset; however, the name actually derives from the Valdôtain dialect, *rouése* meaning glacier.

Punta Gnifetti (Signalkuppe in Swiss German) is famous for having the highest mountain hut, the Cabane Margherita, named after the Queen of Italy, who enjoyed spending her summers in Gressoney-Saint-Jean and the Lys valley. She climbed the mountain and formally opened the hut in August 1893. The hut remains an important part of high-altitude life, and research into high-altitude conditions continues there to this day.

The mountain forming the backdrop of the Lys valley is Lyskamm: it consists of a number of summits and the challenging ridges linking them.

VALTOURNENCHE AND CERVIN/ MATTERHORN

High pastures above Cervinia; the Matterhorn looks on (Route 14)

The small village of Breuil-Cervinia owes its fame and fortune to the dramatic peak at the head of the valley. Cervin is probably most commonly known as the Matterhorn and is, arguably, the most famous mountain in the world. The classic Toblerone view of the mountain is the view from Zermatt, while the Italian side is less well known. The mountain looks just as unclimbable and remains as much of a challenge to mountaineers today as it did during the Golden Age of Mountaineering.

Cervinia provides all the services that would be expected of a modern mountain sports town. There is no shortage of outdoor shops providing for every want and need. There are food shops to stock up on supplies, a multitude of hotels and apartments but, surprisingly, no camp site. A service area for camper vans is located before the town, near the entrance to the road tunnel. A bus route links to the main valley, although this is limited to a few services each day to Chatillon. There is also a TrekBus service, which utilises local taxi firms to transport passengers and/or bags within the valley or to the other lower valleys of Aosta.

Valtournenche is a charming small town on the main road to Cervinia that offers a range of hotels and self-catering options as well as a good campsite, Camping Glair, which has a washing-machine service and Wi-Fi available as well as catering for tents, caravans and campervans.

Two balcony routes start in the village of Cervinia and both end in Valtournenche. Combined, with one route reversed, they could make a lovely two-day trek. Parking in Cervinia can be difficult but if you park in Valtournenche and use the valley bus service to reach the start in Cervinia, the linear routes can be completed without worrying about return transport later in the day. There are several car parks in Valtournenche, usually free of charge. A number of bus stops are located along the main road. (Remember which side of the road you need to be on for the up-valley bus!) These walks start high and finish low, allowing for a gentler day but can be reversed to allow the walker to approach the Matterhorn rather than walk with is as a background feature. To reverse the routes will add to the ascent quite significantly (reverse the decent/ascent) and add an hour to two hours to each walk. Additionally, reversing the routes means the Matterhorn only comes into view in the latter parts of the walks and it also worth being aware that by mid to late morning the summit often begins to be shrouded in mist and cloud.

Map: 1:25,000 Carta dei Sentieri by L'Escursionista Editore 7: Valtournenche, Monte Cervino.

High above the valley of Valtournenche (Route 15)

ROUTE 13

Eastern balcony: Cervinia to Valtournenche

Start	Breuil-Cervinia
Finish	Valtournenche
Distance	13km
Ascent	350m
Descent	840m
Grade	2
Time	5hr 15min

This undulating path provides the Matterhorn as the backdrop to the walk. The Crepin/Salette ski lift, approximately halfway, allows those wishing to enjoy a shorter walk the option to do so, while a nearby high mountain restaurant is a welcome bonus. The charming hamlet of Cheneil offers additional refreshment opportunities. This is a walk that punches above its weight for views!

From the bus station/park in Breuil-Cervinia walk back down the road out of town, taking care to cross onto the left-hand side of the road. Just before the tunnel take the path leftwards leading into a picnic area and continue on to reach the tree adventure course. Pass under the high-wire course and follow the obvious path to reach a road (**15min**).

Follow the road left and uphill around a hairpin bend and on to the next bend. Take Path 107 at the apex of this bend. Follow the dirt track to a signpost and junction (**20min**). ▸

Climb the path, steeply at first, to pass the restaurant of **Baita Layet**. Keep climbing on the vehicle track to a junction (**30min**).

After another five minutes of steep track take Path 107 to the right of the track and climb on rougher ground for a few more minutes before it levels off. ▸

Be sure to keep a look out along the track for the old concrete banked curves of the disused bobsleigh run; the size of the turns is still impressive even in their faded grandeur.

This is a bike park area and it is important to be aware of mountain bikes sharing the trail here.

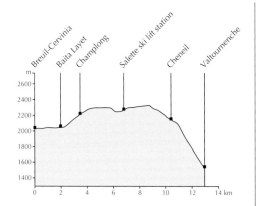

Keep climbing gently to reach an **old railway line** at 2240m, which served the reservoir of Lac Goillet and the more modern water pipe feeding the hydroelectric power station (**1hr 05min**).

After about 300 metres the path becomes a farm track. Follow this to the recently restored chalets at **Champlong** and continue on the track to pass Tsaset and join another track (**1hr 25min**). ▶

A sign here commemorates Pope John-Paul II's meditation visit in July 2000. It is not hard to see how the mountains can encourage reflection and meditation; after all, isn't that part of the reason we all visit?

Leaving Cervinia with the Matterhorn as a backdrop

The lift offers the option of a quick descent to Crepin (Valtournenche), while the nearby restaurant offers a number of good lunch options. It is worth checking that the lift system is operating and the restaurant is open, particularly out of high season.

Continue following the track to the chalets in the near distance at Molar (**1hr 35min**). From here leave the track to follow the path across the hillside. After rounding a shoulder, you will see the Salette ski lift station at Dessert. Descend on the path to join another farm track and follow this to the **ski station** (**2hr 10min**). ◀

From the lift station take the track uphill, passing a junction to the restaurant on the left. Carry on uphill and take the path rather than a track at the next junction. The signs may be somewhat confusing, but a clearly painted '107' on a rock indicates the path is correct. Follow this path, crossing a few streams, to a large cairn, 2355m (**2hr 45min**).

Keep following the obvious path as it crosses some rockier sections to a path junction with Path 27 (**3hr**).

Traverse the hillside with a few small rises to reach the chapel of **Notre-Dame-de-Guérison** above the car

Cheneil with Becca d'Aran towering above

park of Barma, which serves the popular honeypot of **Cheneil** (3hr 30min). ▸

From here you can follow the AV1 into Valtournenche in about an hour and a half. It is advisable to follow the path leftwards from the chapel, Path 26, to Cheneil ((**3hr 45min**)) and then take the well-signed AV1 from there. Leave the hamlet on a steep path to the west, which is clearly signed from the information board. An AV1 sign (a triangle with a 1 inside it) indicates the descent.

Continue down through the trees to pass through a collection of a few houses called Promindoz, which means 'forest clearing' in the local patois; this took place in medieval times to create new farmland. The path becomes a mule track and continues towards Cretaz, part of the village of Valtournenche. The forest gradually changes to hardwoods as you get closer to the valley bottom.

Enter the quaint village of **Cretaz** with its ancient buildings on stone mushrooms, communal laundry sinks and narrow streets barely wide enough for a laden mule! (**5hr 10min**).

The path leads into the lower part of Valtournenche by a large car park. To return to the main part of the village go uphill, rightwards, to reach the cafés and restaurants of Valtournenche (**5hr 15min**).

In Cretaz there is a plaque commemorating the village's most famous son, **Luigi Carrel**, a mountain guide (not to be confused with Jean-Antoine Carrel, the second person to climb the Matterhorn and a contemporary of Whymper). The Carrel name has been associated with mountain guides in Valtournenche from the earliest days of guided exploration to today.

There is a bus service from the car park to Valtournenche. The service is infrequent so times ought to be checked before setting off (the route is timetabled at the bus stops in Valtournenche).

ROUTE 14

Western balcony: Cervinia to Valtournenche

Start	Bus station, Breuil-Cervinia, at the lower end of the town
Finish	Valtournenche
Distance	14km
Ascent	570m
Descent	1100m
Grade	2
Time	5hr 15min

With views of the Italian face of the Matterhorn as a backdrop, this is a spectacular walk. A popular refuge and reasonably short descent (two hours) to Valtournenche mean a long, lingering lunch is possible. The hydroelectric infrastructure and dam are additional interests and the mountainous skyline is a perfect backdrop to a glorious day.

From the bus station in Breuil-Cervinia walk back out of town for a couple of hundred metres towards the tunnel, keep right and cross the large ski bus parking area to reach a small petrol station. Take the road to the right downhill and cross the river. The road enters a new development here. Keep a keen eye out for the path (Path 10) as it ascends to the right. ◀ Keep following Path 10 as it rises across the hillside to a path junction at **Bayettes**, 2291m (**1hr**).

Be careful not to follow Path 107 here; it takes a lower line along the riverside.

From Bayettes follow Path 65 which is something of a balcony path, gaining and dropping in height but broadly maintaining a level route. Cross a number of small streams and pass through old, abandoned chalets to reach a path junction at Bois de Grillon, 2172m (**2hr 10min**). ◀

After heavy rain the balcony path may be impassable as there are no bridges over the streams.

The climb to Fenêtre de Tsignanaz is a reasonably short affair but, for the unacclimatised, it may feel tougher than expected. The high point will be reached

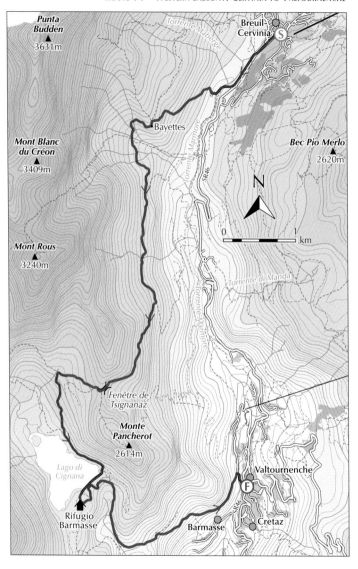

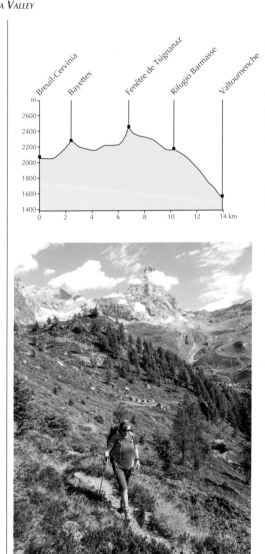

High pastures above Cervinia; the Matterhorn looks on

within about half an hour, **Fenêtre de Tsignanaz**, 2445m **(2hr 40min)**.

Follow the path over the top and, after admiring the view and enjoying a break, begin the descent. Follow the path to reach the farm track and follow this initially rightwards around a hairpin and down past the delightful small church of Madonna di Nevi to the dam wall. Walk across this to reach **Rifugio Barmasse**, 2170m **(3hr 25min)** and a well-earned coffee and cake or indeed an excellent lunch.

From the refuge descend to Valtournenche on the AV1, signposted from the refuge. Take the path which descends below the dam wall and continue down the pass to the impressive remains of the rail access of a hydroelectric scheme, **(4hr 05min)**, and enter the forest and some welcome shade.

Keep following the AV1 signs to pass a shattered rock bastion and signs for the local via ferrata before arriving in Valtournenche. Walk through the small car park, over the bridge and up the incline to arrive in **Valtournenche (5hr 15min)**.

Rifugio Barmasse and Lac Tsignanaz

ROUTE 15
Becca d'Aran

Start/Finish	Car park for Cheneil (Follow signs from Valtournenche for Cheneil; the road is immediately in front of Hôtel Etoile de Neige)
Distance	9km
Ascent	970m
Descent	970m
Grade	2+ (reflects the small amount of steep ground to reach the summit)
Time	4hr 55min

It is hard to beat the view from Becca d'Aran with the vast bulk of the Matterhorn saving itself until the very last moment, the reward for the final short, easy scramble to the summit.

The popular restaurant at Cheneil is a destination for many visitors and provides an afternoon ice cream and refreshment stop. This is a popular summit, with the car park beneath Cheneil filling up quickly; an early start is recommended to ensure a parking place and to reduce the likelihood of the summits being shrouded by afternoon cloud.

Binoculars are a must – there might just be someone summiting the Matterhorn along the knife-edge ridge!

From the car park take the vehicle track, which is signed for Paths 107, 29 and 26; Becca d'Aran is indicated here. You will arrive at a flat spot from which the open, high valley of Cheneil can be admired (**15min**). Drop into the valley to a path junction 50 metres before the obvious bridge.

Take the path left, Path 29/26. Follow this path uphill to reach an abandoned chalet of Aran, 2300m (**1hr**). This sits at the top of a shelf in the valley and makes for a good viewpoint into the valley, as well as a good place for a rest. Keep following this path to a promontory with a small cairn, 2340m (**1hr 15min**).

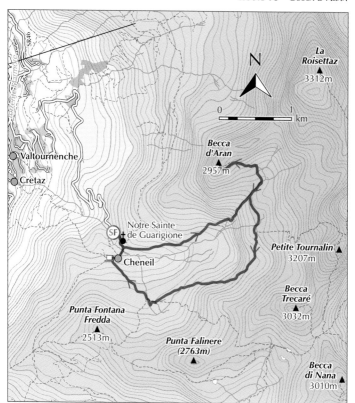

Keep to the path which continues to climb to the left here. Do not be tempted to follow the descending path to the stream.

Cross the stream at 2386m and then climb more directly on the left bank of the stream. Upon reaching an opening in the stream channel, you will reach a path junction. The rightward trending path is marked on the ground as Path 30. The map does not indicate a path number at this point. Keep climbing the path along the line of the stream to gain easier ground, another

123

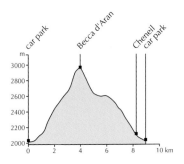

stream-crossing and then a path junction, 2651m (**2hr 15min**).

The path is adequately marked with the usual painted marker lines and has cairns in places but attention to the route is needed.

Cross the stream and follow the path up through open pastures. ◄

Continue a long traverse across the mountainside until a final switch of direction to the right reveals the final summit block. At this altitude the rare edelweiss (*stella alpina* in Italian) is likely to be seen on the sides of the path. You will reach a col before the summit (**2hr 50min**).

The final summit stretch is a simple scramble on good rock, although the continual erosion of the Alpine environment will inevitably mean loose stones will be encountered. Take a line to suit; to the left offers a sportier approach, while an easier route avoiding exposure and most of the hands-on scrambling moves can be found to the right. Within a few minutes you will reach the summit and the most impressive views of the Matterhorn, **Becca d'Aran**, 2957m (**3hr**). ◄

Beware of the significant exposure of the western and northern aspects of the summit, which will either thrill or unnerve; however, there is plenty of space to avoid the exposure and still enjoy the views.

The descent is the same route as the ascent to begin with. Care needs to be taken descending from the summit as the loose stones and angle of the rock require focus and attention but, before long, you will reach the col (**3hr 10min**).

Continue descending on the same path as the ascent to reach the stream basin and crossing point at 2651m (**3hr 30min**). Continue descending along the same route

to reach the **path junction** with Path 30, 10min ((**3hr 40min**)). Take Path 30 (Path 29 on the 1:25,000 map) and climb for a short distance before reaching some high ponds and wetlands (**3hr 45min**).

Continue following the path as it traverses the mountainside and pass numerous small streams to join the AV1 descending from Colle di Nana (**4hr 30min**).

Turn right and downhill to follow the popular AV1 path as it wends its way to **Cheneil**, (**4hr 40min**). Food, drinks and snacks are available here. The path from here to the car park is well marked and popular. The final descent is surprisingly steep, although it is the same path that was climbed first thing in the morning (**4hr 55min**).

The Matterhorn from the summit of Becca d'Aran

VALPELLINE

Trackside woodland provides welcome shade in the heat of the day (Route 19)

The hidden valley of Valpelline, sneaking off from the main Great St Bernard valley, is a real gem; it has a wealth of walks, from short family rambles to long mountain days over the 3000m contour; the AV1 also crosses the valley and makes for a good day's walk.

The shaded and well-equipped campsite in Valpelline (www. grandcombin.com) makes a good base for a week or so's exploring, but it is very popular so booking in advance is recommended. With a swimming pool, games facilities, washing machines, a small shop and a café/restaurant, all the essentials are covered on site. Another good site exists at Lexert, Camping Lac Lexert (www.campinglaclexert.it). It is also well equipped with barbeque areas, laundry facilities, a good restaurant and bar, a small shop and bowling facilities. The small high ropes/tree surfing venue beyond Lexert, Rebel Park, may well be of interest to the younger, or not so young, members of the group. Welcoming hotels, unique refuges and a Fontina cheese visitor centre add to the valley's appeal.

Technically, the area comprises two valleys that converge at Valpelline: the main valley climbs to the large reservoir held in place by an impressive hydroelectric dam. A well-situated refuge at the head of this lake makes for a short walk and a tasty lunch stop. The smaller valley, running north from Valpelline, passes through Ollomont to a tranquil high valley with numerous walks and peaks offering unforgettable views and glimpses of Switzerland, the border being at the head of the valley. This valley has some unusual, ancient, covered waterways used to irrigate the fields; these 'ru' form the basis of two routes here.

Maps: 1:25,000 Carta dei Sentieri by L'Escursionista Editore 6: Valpelline St Bartelemy and 5: Gran St Bernardo, Valle di Ollomont.

ROUTE 16
Rifugio Prarayer

Start/Finish	Car park at Place Moulin Dam – cost: a couple of euros
Distance	9km (or 12.5km)
Ascent	160m (or 230m)
Descent	160m (or 230m)
Grade	1
Time	2hr 20min (or 3hr 20min)

The refuge at Prarayer sits at the head of the long lake of Lac de Place Moulin. The access road is a simple walk of about an hour and is suitable for all sorts of family groups; babies in buggies and older family members will be seen making the journey, along with bounding teenagers and appreciative parents; it's a walk for everyone! The track is also accessible by mountain bike so it is a busy place. This route, taking a higher line, offers a quieter approach and even more impressive views and provides the option of an extension beyond the refuge for those seeking a little more tranquillity.

From the dam wall car park, walk along the obvious vehicle track indicating a myriad of paths. After a couple of hundred metres take the small Path 8 uphill (**5min**).

Climb the path, passing a military pillbox built into the hillside, to reach a farm track 2110m (**30min**). ▸

Follow the farm track/Path 8 (indicating only Rif Nacamuli Col Collon; no mention of Prarayer) to arrive at a large flat area (**35min**). Cross this area to continue on the track.

Keep following the path to reach a junction (**55min**). Go right here (signed Rifugio Prarayer) and descend to a wooden **footbridge** (**1hr**).

Continue for about 100 metres to a path split after the bridge. Take the indicated path, which bears downhill to the right to join the main access track. Pass through

The route ahead can be seen as it undulates through the high alpages to a bridge over Torrente d'Oren about 2km away.

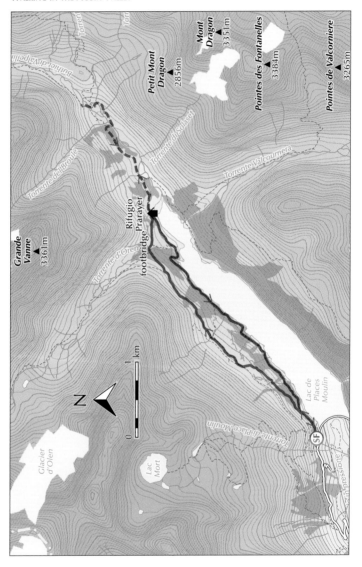

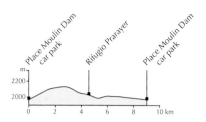

the hamlet of Prarayer to reach **Rifugio Prarayer (1hr 20min).** ▶

The return to the car park is a little over an hour, via the access track along the edge of the lake, and is a simple walk.

The refuge offers a fine lunch menu based on local ingredients and is very popular in high season.

Possible extension

For those wishing to extend the walk there appears to be a loop of about 3km utilising Paths 9,10 and 11 to Gordzè. Unfortunately, at the time of writing, the bridge at spot height 2027m was not a safe crossing. Path 9 was closed

The views from Rifugio Prarayer are well worth the walk

129

The old Path 9 is evident 100 metres before the turn downhill to the bridge; it is blocked. The unsafe bridge is visible at the bend of the path. If it has been rebuilt/repaired it will be obvious at this point.

on the approach to the bridge and the bridge itself was far from safe: there were missing planks and no handrail.

However, all is not lost; an interesting extension can be followed which will take around an hour and offer some interesting sights:

Follow the signs for Path 10 along the track and then, at Grand Plan, this track becomes a smaller path. Descend to a well-built wooden bridge that crosses the river (**1hr 40min**). ◄

Cross the bridge and follow the path leftwards to another bridge and on to a third bridge (**1hr 55min**).

After this bridge a wooden sign indicates a 'monumental tree'. This old larch tree, which is protected, is over 500 years old and is certainly of considerable size compared to the surrounding trees (**2hr**).

The blue-purple flowers that grow along the path here are **monkshood**, a poisonous plant which was used in ancient times to poison arrow heads and blades. It is contact poisonous and may result in numbness or nausea. Do not touch this plant; admire it from afar!

Alternatively, you can follow Path 11 as far as Alpe Betta Tsa, passing impressive waterfalls en route. This will take approximately 55 minutes from the second bridge and path junction.

To return, retrace your steps to Prarayer, about 20 minutes, and continue on to the car park, another hour.

The ancient larch, at least 500 years old and still in good health

ROUTE 17

Ru di-z-Aagne and Fontina

Start	Chozod-Semon
Finish	Ollomont (or Valpelline)
Distance	5 km
Ascent	300m
Descent	30m
Grade	1
Time	1hr 45min

Ru were built to manage water supplies before the advent of pumps and hosepipes. They are usually covered small-sized 'canals' with some open sections. They keep water flowing at a gentle rate, and they make for very pleasant walking on near-level paths and this is no exception.

This short walk offers dappled shade as it follows an ancient water course through the forests to reach the Fontina cheese visitor centre. This traditionally produced cheese is a feature of many local dishes.

From the main road (no nearby parking; there is a bus service, bus stop 'Chozod-Semon') take the road into the village of Semon to reach the small church of Cappella di San Rocco (**15min**).

From the church, take the road uphill out of the village, passing interesting village gardens en route to reach the Ru di-z-Aagne, an irrigation channel (**30min**). The path is signed from the church as Path 3B. As the track climbs it bears left to pass a water-treatment building. Red signs for the ru help to keep you on the correct path. ▶

Follow the ru through the forest, passing the large water pipes feeding the power station in Valpelline, to reach the road to Ollomont (**40min**). Take the road left (downhill) for about 100 metres to a junction with a minor road (**45min**). Take this minor road (right), which is signed for the **Centro Visita Fontina**.

In late summer the keen forager ought to be able to collect blackberries along the way.

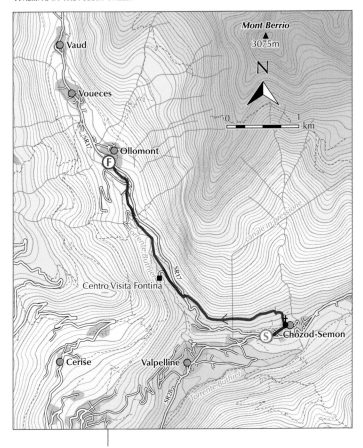

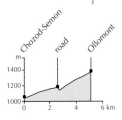

Tracing its origins to the 1700s, **Fontina cheese** is a speciality of the Aosta valley and is made from the unpasteurised milk of the red-brown-and-white Valdostana cows typically seen on the mountain pastures. It is quite a creamy, strong-flavoured cheese, suitable for fondue.

Follow this towards a road junction, Frissonière **(50min)**. Walk down to the centre, a must for all cheese lovers. Back at the Frissonière road junction, take the track to a small chapel on the right. Follow this track as it climbs steadily, passing the chapel of St Agostino to reach **Ollomont (1hr 35min)**. ▸

It is possible to return to Valpelline in about half an hour from the Frissonière junction by taking Path 2 leftwards and downhill. This is the old road and brings you into the village via the school and another small church, Notre Dame aux Neiges. ▸

An occasional bus service operates from Ollomont to Valpelline. Check in Valpelline before setting out. Alternatively, you can follow the same path back to Valpelline in about one hour.

A small shop (also a café) sells essential supplies, including maps, snacks and sandwiches.

Take time to notice the Virgin Mary depicted among snow fields.

Approaching Ollomont along the old road

ROUTE 18
Lac Mort

Start/Finish	Car park at Place Moulin Dam. Cost: a couple of euros
Distance	7.5km
Ascent	1050m
Descent	1050m
Grade	2
Time	3hr 45min

Starting from the immense hydroelectric dam, and passing an unusual monorail that climbs its way up the mountainside to a remote chalet, this walk is full of surprises. Lac Mort (Lago Morto) occupies a wild and remote spot that has the feel of somewhere much higher than its 2800m altitude might suggest. Even in the middle of summer the lake is a mix of icebergs and cool blue water. The moon-like landscape further enhances the other-worldly feel of the high altitude. Far-reaching views are another reward for the climb up into the higher mountains.

From the busy car park area take the road which climbs up the hillside. This quickly becomes a track with several hairpin bends to aid the ascent. After 100m altitude gain take Path 7 signposted "Lago Morto, 2h 10min." (**15min**). ◄

This is a pretty steep section of the walk as it climbs the hillside quite directly, the advantage being that height and therefore views improve equally quickly.

Climb the hill on the path which follows the line of the stream, to join another path emerging from the left at a path junction (**40min**). Broken tree trunks will probably be encountered along here, clear evidence of the power of the spring avalanches that sweep these slopes, hence the limited tree growth.

From here the views of the dam and the beautiful blue lake are worth pausing for.

Turn right onto the waymarked path and climb steeply to pass the obvious rock bastion and continue on to a flatter section, where the path contours the hillside in a rising traverse (**55min**). ◄

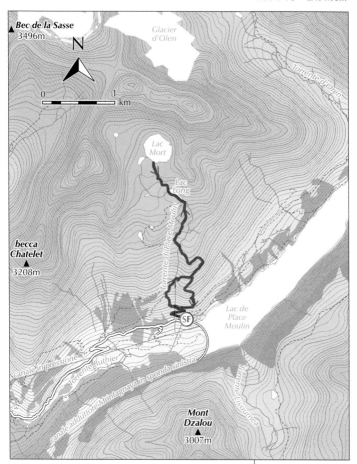

The water of **Lac de Place Moulin** has such a striking blue colour because very fine sediment from glacial meltwater (known as rock flour) is held in suspension in the water. This sediment absorbs the red part of the spectrum and reflects the blue, intensifying the colour.

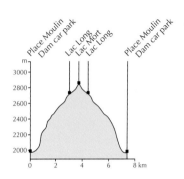

This monumental feat of engineering serves the summer chalets higher up the mountain.

Continue along the obvious path until you reach an unusual **monorail track**. ◄ Follow the path which shadows the monorail to a path junction. Take the path rightwards, signed 'Lac Long' and arrive at some chalets (**1hr 25min**).

Follow the path to the lovely waterfalls below Lac Long, 2720m (**2hr**). Lac Mort is not too far from here. Keep on the obvious path with **Lac Long** on your right.

Lac Long reflecting the mountains in perfect calm

Take a moment to marvel at the view of the mountains reflected in the lake behind you before climbing the final slopes to Lac Mort. The path becomes less distinct but continues to climb over a small shoulder to reach the glacial **Lac Mort**, 2843m (**2hr 15min**).

The return is by the same path, although it is also feasible to visit the small Lac de la Tête and Lac de Mont Ross from Lac Long by taking the path to the right at the top end of the lake. There is also an option of following the path (also Path 7) more directly downhill from the plateau where the monorail is located. This wends a line down the hillside, passing the abandoned chalets at Le Meà, which were constructed in 1923 according to a date inscribed in a roof beam. Pass the anti-avalanche construction, which protects the dam from winter snow, to join a track by a tunnel and the terminal of the monorail. Follow this track left back to the **car park**. Either return route will take around an hour and a half (**3hr 45min**).

The remarkable monorail allows farmers to access the high chalets easily

137

ROUTE 19

Ru du Rey: a marvel of hydro-engineering

Start/Finish	Rey, car park
Distance	14km
Ascent	710m
Descent	710m
Grade	2
Time	4hr 40min

At the remote head of the Ollomont valley the Ru du Rey brings water to the farms in the lower valley. At one time this was a vital source of water but, with the introduction of powered water pumps, the ru has become less important, although it still provides water to communities in the high mountains. This particularly well-engineered section (approximately 6km in length) is exciting as it takes to mesh walkways above the water.

The day begins with about 20 minutes of quiet road walking to reach the hamlet of **Vaud**.

At Vaud take the old road through the hamlet and rejoin the 'main road'. Within 100 metres identify the path leaving the road to the right and follow this. Cross the bridge and take the path leftwards which climbs into the trees. Follow the path to reach the farm of Crottes, 1591m (**35min**). Just before the farm take the left fork of the path and descend to **Glassier**, 1533m (**40min**). ◄

There is a café here for refreshments.

Take the road to the left for approximately 200 metres to a track leaving the road to the right. Be careful to take the right path here; the correct route is signed 'Bivacco Savoia' not the one signed 'Paths 3, 4, 5a, 5b'.

Our route initially ascends a dirt track around three hairpins. After the third hairpin take the path uphill, signed Path 3, which leaves the track. Climb quite steeply for a short while with ever-improving views into

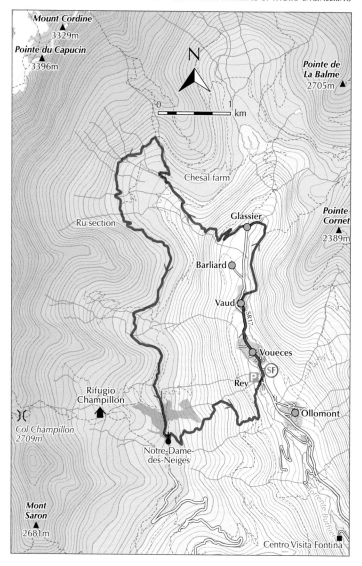

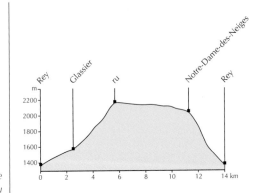

A family enjoying the views from the ru

the valley. Before long, you will reach the treeline and enter the small valley of the Torrente Berruard. Keep on the path as it climbs towards the farm. Take the path as it veers left before the farm and continue to follow the stream to reach a farm track, 2000m (**1hr 45min**).

Follow the track left and having crossed the stream, turn right on Path 3, which follows the farm track to access the farm of **Chesal**. From here the path climbs the open pastures to reach a visible track running along the mountainside. This is the beginning of the ru, 2167m (**2hr 10min**).

Follow the clear path left as it contours around the mountainside. ▸

The ru is covered, in the most part, to protect the water from evaporation. It follows a gently descending line along the mountainside. After a few minutes a rope handrail helps along a short, exposed section lasting only a few minutes. ▸

Continue along the ru around the bowl of the Comba Berruard, crossing a few **small streams**, until a short distance beyond the hairpin bends by Ècondu a seemingly impossible cliff bars the way; the ru enters a fissure in the cliff via a small metal bridge, (**2hr 50min**). Pass through this impressive piece of engineering.

The path becomes more of a track in the **larch forests**. After approximately 20 minutes a large track climbs to meet and cross the ru. Keep following the path as it contours around another bowl and enters some trees. There is another short section of metal walkway and then the ru is uncovered. The tumbling ice-cold water is a refreshing partner as it leads the way to the farm of Champillon, 2050m (**3hr 15min**). ▸

Follow the track to the small church of **Notre-Dame-des-Neiges** (**3hr 20min**).

From here the route follows the AV1 down to Rey, signed with triangles with a number 1 inside. The path is initially quite steep. Follow this towards the cow sheds and then bear right, downhill. Following the path here is tricky due to the number of cow tracks. After about 10

The waymarking identifies this as part of the TDC, the Tour Des Combins, a long-distance trek of around 100km.

The views of the twin summits of Grand Combin and Mont Gelé are particularly impressive along this section.

Signs invite the walker to visit Rifugio Champillon along this section of the path; the food, views and welcome at the refuge may well tempt many walkers. This will add an hour of ascent and another 40 minutes of descent to the day.

The ru enters a dramatic and well-engineered rock chasm

minutes the path's entrance into the forest is visible to the left of the lower part of the meadow.

Enter the forest and follow the good path as it passes several abandoned chalets in the forest to a path junction. Turn left then right almost immediately. The path emerges from the forest behind the Locanda delle Miniere, where ice creams and drinks are available all day. The **car park** is a few minutes down the road (**4hr 40min**).

ROUTE 20
Pointe Cornet

Start/Finish	Rey, car park
Distance	13km
Ascent	1050m
Descent	1050m
Grade	2
Time	4hr 50min

Pointe Cornet is an achievable peak; it is not a technical ascent but it gives a feeling of real achievement as well as far-reaching views, including a sneak peek into Switzerland towards the col of Fenêtre de Durand: an old smuggling route and the pass used by the Italian president to escape Nazi persecution after the Italian armistice in 1943.

Climbing up from the inhabited valley through woodland and high mountain pastures to reach the *pays sauvage* (wild country) provides real experience of the changes that occur as altitude takes effect.

Having parked in the ample car park, head back to the road (signed for the AV1 to Oyace) and follow it back down the valley for 200 metres. Take the road off to the left, signposted to Cognein (**3min**). After three more minutes take the track that takes the hill directly, still the AV1. A small fire hydrant occupies this junction (**5min**).

Follow this track/road directly uphill, crossing the road again. The track becomes rougher and begins to zig-zag its way up the hillside in wooded shade to eventually reach a more open section that offers views down the valley (**55min**). Keep following the track (this is the farm access track so occasionally you may meet vehicles), cross a small stream and then follow the track as it follows the stream course in Comba de Berrio to arrive at the farm of **Berrio Dessus**, 1926m (**1hr 45min**).

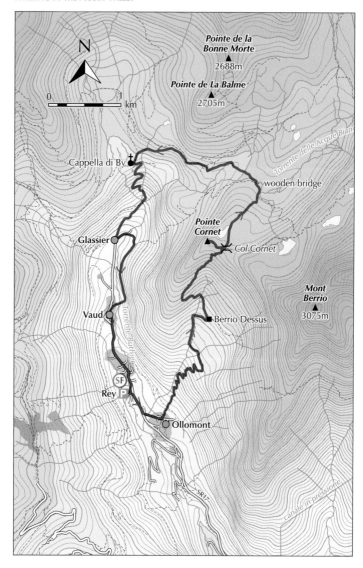

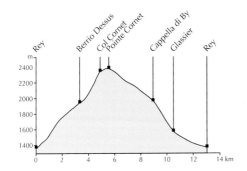

From the farm take the path to the left of the buildings, which climbs into the broad valley. The summit of Pointe Cornet is visible almost directly ahead, but the path works across the slope in a large zigzag to reach **Col Cornet**, 2358m **(2hr 55min)**. ▶

The **view from the col** is well worth a moment. Jagged summits form a magnificent backdrop and lead around to Mont Gelé (literally 'Frozen Mountain') and its rapidly retreating glacier. The eagle-eyed will see *stella alpina* growing nearby (more commonly known as edelweiss). Remember these are a protected and rare species and should be admired; take only photographs.

The summit is a short distance from here with little ascent. The large iron cross is typical of Alpine summits, **Pointe Cornet**, 2389m **(3hr 05min)**. ▶

There are numerous options from here: the most obvious is to trace the ascent route; this will take around an hour and a half. Another option is to go via the Cappella di By and the café at Glassier.

This second option requires a little route finding as the path is indistinct in places but the general direction is obvious. Begin by returning to the col and take the left path, which drops to Lac Cornet and then follows the

You will see a wealth of alpine flowers along this section, including Alpine rose (wild roses), Alpenrose (wild, small rhododendron) and mountain aster.

Binoculars will be useful for viewing the mountains and valleys and will allow you to observe the mighty Grand Combin (4314m); a remote and difficult-to-reach summit means it is one of the less frequented Alpine 4000ers.

The summit cross of Pointe Cornet

stream from this high post-glacial cirque to a junction with Path 6 (signed with painted circles) in the broad valley below, 2230m (**3hr 25min**).

Follow the path, making sure to cross the stream on a small **wooden bridge** before the obvious small dam (**3hr 30min**). This is Path 6A which continues to Balme de Bal where it meets a track.

Follow the track as it contours the valley for 400 metres and take Path 5, which drops to the left of the track (**3hr 35min**).

This path descends the hillside to join another track a few hundred metres before the chapel. This is the Path of Hope (Le Sentier de l'Espoir) and was an often-used track to and from Switzerland.

The path is most famously known in Italy as the route **Luigi Einaudi** took to escape to Switzerland and avoid persecution following the fall of the fascist regime in Italy in 1943. He returned to Italy to govern the national bank and, eventually, became the second president of the Italian Republic in 1948. He is remembered for his belief in the

The verdant forests of the lower valley, departing Glassier

European Federation and in neo-liberal thinking. After retiring from political life, he managed a very successful vineyard, producing Nebbiolo wine.

After regaining the track, the short diversion to the **Cappella di By**, to see a traditional high pasture summer chapel with its simple décor, is worthwhile, 1987m (**3hr 50min**).

Our descent route involves a reasonably direct path down the hillside in a series of zigzags. This path enters the wooded shade of the summer forests (keep an eye out for tiny but delicious wild strawberries) and eventually becomes a well-maintained walled path to reach a path junction (**4hr 15min**). Crossing a delightful bridge en route, Paths 3,4 and 5 all follow the same descent to **Glassier** (**4hr 25min**).

From here two options present themselves. Following the road back to Rey is one option. Alternatively, you can follow a path from the café (Path 6) as it passes the large cow shed at Crottes and enters the forest. Do not take the uphill path at the junction. The route is a gentle, descending line that follows the river course but in delightfully shaded woodland. Exit the woods to cross a wooden bridge and enter the village of **Vaud** (**4hr 40min**). Take the old road through the heart of the village and join the valley road for the last 10 minutes of walking to reach **Rey** (**4hr 50min**).

ROUTE 21

Alta Via 1: Col de Breuson

Start	Les Sergnoux bus stop, Closé
Finish	Ollomont
Distance	11km
Ascent	1080m
Descent	1150m
Grade	2
Time	5hr 15min

The valley buses make this stage of the AV1 (The Giants' Trail) a single day's expedition. The AV1 is a two-week trek 'across the grain' of the northern valleys, involving almost 180km and 14,000m of ascent. This walk is a full stage of the trek and gives a feel of the challenge. Crossing the Col de Breuson may bring walkers into close contact with eagles cruising the thermals rising from the mountain ridges above. The two Alpine kings are your companions for the day: the Matterhorn acts as a backdrop to the climb and Mont Blanc is visible from the summit. The Gran Paradiso National Park is also clearly visible from the col. Don't forget binoculars!

From Valpelline a bus runs up the valley in the early morning, around 8am (check bus stops for the correct timings). The most suitable starting point then is Closé, above the village of Oyace. The hardest route finding of the day will probably be identifying the correct departure point from the huddle of settlements in Closé–Oyace.

From the bus stop at Les Sergnoux, Closé, follow the cobbled track that leaves the main road and climbs directly up the slope to join the track from Condamine farm. ▶

Turn left at this junction and continue along the road until a sign on the right indicates the AV1 leaves to the right uphill (**10min**).

Continue along this path as it initially climbs the hillside before traversing left (west) to cross a gully, which shows evidence of winter avalanches (**25min**).

Painted race arrows from various trail races are usually evident on the road here.

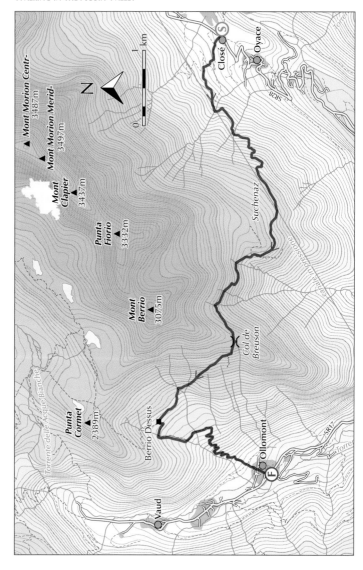

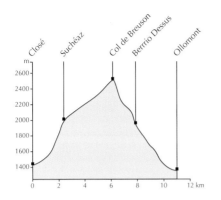

After the gully follow the path that climbs up to **Suchéaz**, 1995m (**1hr 15min**). ▶

Continue following the path through the forest until you reach a small clearing at 2100m and views of Monte Emilius (3559m), a fine, pointed peak across the main

Views of the Matterhorn and also the less well-known Dent d'Hérens can be had here, and it is a good place for the first break of the day.

The view from the col is impressive, with Monte Emilius in the distance

It is possible to use Path 3C as an escape route to Valpelline, should you need to make a diversion.

Aosta valley. Continue to a **path junction** with Path 3C, and some old chalets at Breson l'Arpe, 2200m (**1hr 55min**). A sign indicating Col de Breuson as being 40 minutes away is optimistic for most walkers. ◄

As you reach **Col de Breuson**, 2508m, (**2hr 45min**), the views are breathtaking. Grand Combin, Mont Blanc and Monte Emilius are just three of the summits that are clearly visible. Eagles and vultures soaring high above may well be your companions along this stretch. The col also makes for a fine lunch stop.

The descent from here is via a path that tackles what appear to be alarmingly steep slopes. Fortunately, the path wends a gentler, but longer, route. ◄ Follow the path, taking care at 2450m to ensure that you are still following the AV1. An alternative 'dead end' path leads

Soil creep is particularly evident in the numerous natural terraces on this slope.

Approaching the high farm of Berrio Dessus

nowhere. Ollomont and Rey are visible far below. At around 2200m the path levels off, which will be a relief for complaining knees! A wooden table and chairs here make for a welcome break (**3hr 20min**).

Follow the path as it traverses the hillside and cross a boulder field (which may have avalanche-felled trees to clamber over) and join a farm track which descends towards the farm of **Berrio Dessus** (Berrio Damon on the map), 1932m (**4hr 20min**).

As you approach, aim for about 100 metres to the right of the farm and join a track descending left to the actual farm buildings and then take the vehicle track.

Follow the farm access track to cross a couple of streams and enter the forest and continue descending to the valley via a series of hairpins.

When you reach a small road, cross it and follow the track directly downhill into **Ollomont** (**5hr 15min**). ▶

There is a small café in the centre of Ollomont.

There is a bus service back to Valpelline from Ollomont; again, checking timings prior to tackling the walk is advised as the services tend to run only in the early and later part of the day. Alternatively, there is a path to Valpelline, Path 2, which was once a pack horse route and takes around an hour. It leaves Ollomont opposite the church at the lower end of the village.

Looking down on the Valpelline valley far below

153

ROUTE 22
Rifugio and Col Champillon

Start/Finish	Car park at Plan Détruit (Plan Debat on the map)
Distance	4.5km (or 6.5km if going to the col)
Ascent	360m (plus 275m to the col)
Descent	360m (plus 275m to the col)
Grade	1 (2 if carrying on to the col)
Time	1hr 35min (3hr including the col)

Col Champillon is a popular walk for adventurous families looking for a significant viewpoint and a lovely lunch spot. The views from Col Champillon reach as far as Mont Blanc. The balcony and veranda of Rifugio Champillon offer an impressive lunch viewpoint along with local specialities and various natural health remedies, making it a destination in itself. Should you wish to enjoy the health and spa facilities, it is necessary to book in advance.

As the walk has two options, part of the group may wish to walk as far as the refuge and form a 'base camp' on the balcony while some venture on to the col; it's around an hour and a half additional walking for the round trip.

Although it is usually locked, a curious peek through the barred windows shows a beautifully decorated interior.

The local Fontina cheese can be purchased here.

From the car park a rough vehicle track leads to the small chapel of Notre-Dame-des-Neiges (**10min**). ◄

Continue following the vehicle track, taking care to take the rising track to the left after around 100 metres or so, clearly signed to the refuge. Follow this track as it climbs to the farm at Pessinoille (**20min**).

From here take the steeper path which leaves the track and cuts off a large track bend. Cross the track again and continue climbing the hillside to reach the pictur-esque farm of Isa (2297m) (**45min**). ◄

The refuge is close by but remains hidden from view. Follow the vehicle track for about 400 metres until a path leaves it to climb the hillside. Take this path and,

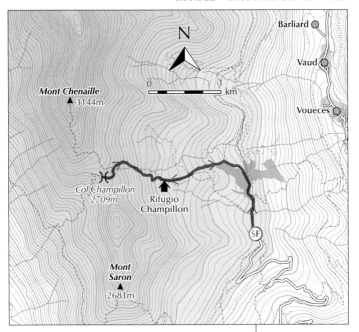

before too long, the refuge comes into sight. **Rifugio Champillon**, 2465m (**1hr**). ▶

With a variety of wellness services on site, from saunas and massage to yoga and Pilates, it is not your typical refuge. www. rifugio-champillon.it

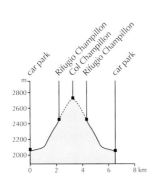

The eagle-eyed will spot **Fenêtre de Durand**, a pass north-east of the refuge in the distance. This marks the Swiss border and was used as an escape route to Switzerland by the Italian president, Luigi Einaudi, during World War 2 when fleeing Nazi persecution after the Italian armistice in 1943.

For those wishing to climb to the col, the path is obvious. Take the signed path, keeping an eye out for eagles soaring on the late morning thermals. The path is well worn and easy to follow. As the path levels off, you will pass an intriguing standing stone with a hole through it. Mont Blanc will make a welcome appearance

Approaching Rifugio Champillon

and the summit is reached. **Col Champillon** (2709m) (**1hr 50min**).

Return by simply retracing the ascent route, which is about 35 minutes from the col and another 35 minutes from the refuge to the **car park** (**1hr 35min (3h including the return route to the col)**).

Trekkers relaxing at Rifugio Champillon after climbing from the valley floor, a hard 1100m ascent

GREAT SAINT BERNARD PASS

Looking down to the Grand Col du St Bernard from Col de St Rhémy (Route 25)

Travellers have used the col as a crossing point for thousands of years and, no doubt, will continue to do so. Bronze Age artefacts have been found in the area. The Romans developed the top of the col, constructing a temple and other buildings to support travellers, providing them with a means of giving thanks for a successful ascent and asking for a guiding hand in descent.

With the total crossing reaching close to 80km, a 'halfway house' has always been essential for travellers. Benedictine monks have provided shelter and sustenance for travellers at the summit of the pass since AD1049. Initially, the hospice was established to provide safe passage for pilgrims and travellers from bandits; the role of search and rescue evolved as a natural result of the climate and altitude. The pass climbs nearly 2000m from both Aosta and Martigny, the 'book-end' towns of the pass, to a high point of 2469m. Snow can fall at any time of the year and can lie up to 10m deep in winter; temperatures have been recorded as low as -30°C. The approach from the Swiss side is particularly susceptible to avalanches; with such extremes and such a long distance to cross it is hardly a surprise that the Combe des Morts and Mont Mort lie on the route.

Étroubles is the first of the real mountain settlements encountered on the journey to the col and has been reborn as an outdoor art museum. There is a trail of outdoor artwork around the village to admire and contemplate; in the summer there is usually a range of temporary exhibitions to enjoy too.

The villages which evolved to offer accommodation and support for the crossing still offer a range of accommodation options along with a few campsites. Of historical importance is Château Verdun at

St Oyen, an old staging post for the arduous crossing of the col, owned and managed by the monastery and popular with those completing the Via Francigena. Camping Mulino (no website) and Camping Pineta (www.campingbarpineta.it) sit in pleasant valley-bottom sites. Both offer basic facilities, including laundry and small café/restaurant services. There is a camper van pull-off area at a hairpin bend about 2km up the pass from Saint-Rhémy-en-Bosses. This space is a popular overnight stop with plenty of capacity. A van sells bread, cheese and dried meats there each day too.

A few accommodation options are available at the col itself. The hospice primarily caters for trekkers and travellers and offers mountain-hut-style services (www.gsbernard.com), while the adjacent hotel offers an upmarket experience (www.aubergehospice.ch). The Albergo Italia (www.gransanbernardo.it) is close by, on the Italian side of the pass, and offers a traditional hotel experience and restaurant.

Map: 1:25,000 Carta dei Sentieri by L'Escursionista Editore 5: Gran St Bernardo, Valle di Ollomont.

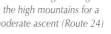

The summit of Mont Fourchon gives the feeling of being in the high mountains for a moderate ascent (Route 24)

159

ROUTE 23

Via Francigena to Great St Bernard Monastery

Start	Saint-Oyen
Finish	Great St Bernard Monastery
Distance	11km
Ascent	1160m
Descent	30m
Grade	2
Time	4hr 30min

To walk in the footsteps of pilgrims to one of the most famous monasteries in the world is certainly a journey through time. From Château Verdun to the monastery is one of the most challenging sections of the pilgrims' road. Every step of the way echoes with the feet of the countless travellers who have journeyed between Canterbury and Rome. The final approach follows the far older Roman road and passes the remains of Roman temples. And then into view comes the enormous monastery. The equally famous St Bernard dogs are kennelled here and a small museum explains the evolution of the hospice, the monastery and the travellers crossing the Alps.

A bus service from the monastery returns to Saint-Rhémy-en-Bosses and Saint-Oyen. It is worth checking timings as the service is infrequent and there may well be a couple of hours between buses. Alternatively, start by parking a car at the monastery and take the bus to Saint-Oyen (www.savda.it).

Château Verdun was a staging post on the Road to Rome Pilgrimage, and it maintains a role in providing accommodation to travellers today. It offers small rooms and *dortoirs* (dormitories) to travellers on foot or in vehicles. The building is peaceful, reflecting the religious nature of the Via Francigena. Although it is in Italy, Château Verdun is owned by

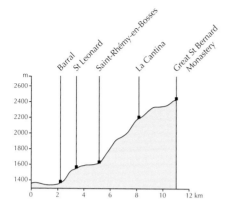

the monastery. In previous times the changing of mules and horses would have been a key function of the *château* as well as providing rest and recuperation for guides and those patrolling the pass to keep bandits at bay.

The road is busy as it is the road to Switzerland. Follow it uphill out of the village, keeping an eye out for the signs for Path 103. It leaves the road to the left at the end of the village, (Via Francigena) (**5min**).

Follow the path down to the valley bottom and along the track to emerge at La Barral (**40min**).

Turn right onto a road and begin to climb steadily uphill. Be careful to follow the 103 signs at the first major bend into the hamlet of **St Leonard**. After ascending a flight of steps take time to appreciate the large stained-glass panel commemorating the Via Francigena at the small plaza (**1hr**).

Keep on up through the houses still following signage for Path 103 and the ancient track which traverses the hillside to reach **Saint-Rhémy-en-Bosses**. Cross the bridge and then turn left to continue on the old road, which is the 'main street' in Saint-Rhémy-en-Bosses (**1hr 20min**). ▶

Be sure to note the tops of the lamp posts with a pilgrim on his journey to Rome.

161

SWITZERLAND

Pointe de Drône
2949m

Tête de Fonteinte
2775m

Grande Chenalette
2900m

Great St Bernard Monastery ✝ Ⓕ

La Cantina

Tete De Barasson

ITALY

Torrente del Gran San Bernardo

Monte Pag
2476r

Torrente di Barasson

N

0   1 km

T2

Saint-Rhémy-en-Bosses

SS27

Eter De

T2

St Leonard

Saint-Oyen

Torrente Artanavaz

Torrente di Flassin

Tete du Bois de Quart
2249m

Trekkers in Saint-Rhémy-en-Bosses contemplating the Via Francigena to the monastery

Head up out of the village passing a small church and statue of the Madonna. The pilgrim road joins the modern road for about 300 metres before leaving it on the right. Cross the road with care. Climb the hillside on Path 103 at a steeper gradient than the road. ▶

Be careful not to follow Path 13, which climbs even more steeply.

Path 103 is obviously an old road and displays interesting well-engineered sections as it climbs across the mountainside. A few zigzags climb the hillside and the path signs change to 13B and the TDC. The pilgrim's road is obvious and continues climbing towards the col. Keep climbing and pass a cave with a plaque commemorating the Stagnini gypsies' use of the cave to shelter from snowstorms (**2hr 40min**).

Continue following the path until you meet Path 13 (**2hr 55min**).

PATOU DOGS

There are often warnings about *patou* dogs at work in the area. These are large white shepherding dogs used to protect flocks from wolves and other predators. Should you have an encounter:

- Stop, preferably together as a group
- Remain calm and quiet; allow the dogs to assess you
- Do not shout, run or wave sticks or maps at them; you won't frighten them off and you might provoke them to attack
- If you have a dog, keep it on a lead and close by
- When the dogs (there are usually two) have lost interest in you, walk calmly and quietly past the flock

Although a path is marked on the map as taking a much shorter line to the hospice, this is not a feasible path. the TDC/Via Francigena path is far more suitable.

Notice the beasts he has overcome and chained at his feet, thereby making the crossing safe.

Turn left and follow the path (Path 13) up the valley towards the road as the path crosses the road at **La Cantina**, 2210m (**3hr 05min**). Cross the road and pastures to cross the road once more. ◀

Continue following the waymarks across the high pastures towards the impressive galleried road ahead. Before reaching this, traverse rightwards at a signposted path junction to join the road after the gallery section (**3hr 55min**).

Cross the road carefully, as there is a blind bend here, and follow the Roman road through a carved-out section to reach the statue of St Bernard. ◀ The path drops to join the road and the first of the tourist stalls selling the ubiquitous St Bernard cuddly dogs are encountered. Follow the road or, if it is open, the lakeside path to the monastery. To cross from Italy into Switzerland is little more than crossing a stream over a small bridge as the customs post seems to be permanently closed. However, a passport is still an essential travel document! (**4hr 10min**)

Arriving at the **Great St Bernard Monastery** (2469m) (**4hr 30min**) is somewhat bewildering. Buses, motorbikes, supercars, cyclists and walkers all vie for position on the road and for tables in the bars and cafés. The actual hospice is on the right on the approach; the kennels and museum are to the left along with the hotel entrance. To think that the door has been open to travellers in need of assistance for over 1000 years is truly humbling. In summer there is a flight of 11 steps to the door; in winter ski tourers can ski straight to the door.

THE GREAT ST BERNARD MONASTERY

The monastery comes into view for a trekking group

St Bernard founded the monastery in 1049AD to help travellers struggling over the high pass between Italy and Switzerland. Many fell foul of the weather; the nearby Combe des Morts gives a clue as to how desperate early or late season crossings could be. The first building encountered from the Swiss side was the mortuary, used to store all those unfortunate souls recovered over the winter, ready to be buried in spring when the pass allowed travel down to the valley churches and consecrated ground. Even today it is a dangerous crossing in winter requiring good mountain skills and a knowledge of the area.

The frequent winter accidents and avalanches meant the monks were, effectively, the world's first mountain rescue team. They developed a breed of dog well suited to searching and recovering those lost or injured; the St Bernard was born.

The dogs are no longer used as routine search and rescue dogs; helicopters and smaller, more agile breeds fulfil this role. However, the dogs remain a strong aspect of life at the col and the kennels welcome visitors each day.

Probably the most famous traveller to cross the col is Napoleon. He passed through with 40,000 troops. Although in reality he crossed astride a mule, the iconic painting by Jacques Louis David depicts Napoleon mounted on a rearing stallion pointing onwards. The nearby village of Bourg-Saint-Pierre was issued a promissory note by Napoleon to pay for food and supplies as part of this crossing. The debt remained unpaid until the French President, François Mitterrand, visited in 1983 and settled the outstanding bill.

From here Canterbury and Rome are pretty much equidistant, both being about 1000km away. The Via Francigena is a long walk, taking pilgrims three to four months to complete; many complete sections each year over a period of time.

For those looking to extend their walk it is possible to return to Saint-Oyen in around three hours.

Following the ancient road to Rome through St Remy en Bosses

ROUTE 24
Mont Fourchon

Start/Finish	Baou: rough car park next to farm on road from Aosta (SS27)
Distance	4km
Ascent	550m
Descent	550m
Grade	2+ (reflects a rougher path to the actual summit)
Time	3hr 15min

The summit of Mont Fourchon, hidden from the road, allows the adventurous walker to experience a superlative viewpoint of two Alpine giants: Grand Combin and Mont Blanc. A rough final section adds to the adventure; at no point does the path become a scramble but in places it will be necessary to use a hand, or even both, to aid balance and upward momentum. Herds of *bouquetin* (Alpine ibex) and chamois may be encountered, as might the ptarmigan (known as *le lagopède* in French; *pernice bianca* in Italian) among the rocks. In the later summer months, the birds will be changing to their winter plumage. The route has a high starting point, at nearly 2400m, which means the lofty summit of 2902m is attained without too much effort.

The walk begins from a popular car parking spot at a bend in the road not long before the galleried road section. Unusually, there is no signpost offering suggestions of times or destinations. The path is well worn and takes a diagonal rising line to the left of the car park.

Take the path, which is surprisingly rough and rocky, as it traverses the hillside. It begins to zigzag its way up the hillside and twists and turns its way up, gaining height quite quickly, to reach a **path junction** with Path 13A (**30min**). ▶

Follow Path 13C which leaves the more travelled route and climbs leftwards. Signs on the rocks are reassuring. The gradient eases as you reach a small pond that

The impressive Tour des Fous rock formation dominates the walk.

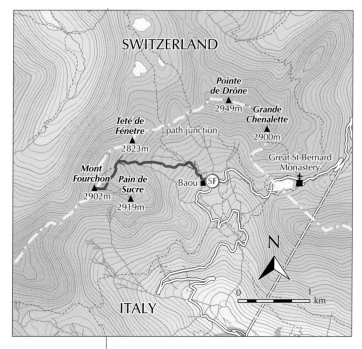

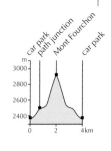

offers beautiful reflections of the surrounding mountains. The Tour des Fous is now below the path and is just as impressive from above as from below. Continue following the path towards the cwm with snow patches ahead.

Traverse rightwards across the grassy slope (still following the path). The path becomes less distinct and you need to keep an eye on the ground for the occasional painted marker and the more frequent cairns to a less distinct path junction, 2725m **(50min)**.

Take the path leftwards here. Beware of another path, also cairned, continuing ahead; this leads to a small col on the skyline and a more difficult route along the skyline ridge, which is probably grade 2 scrambling (marked on the map as a grey line). For

the correct route follow the cairned path in a southerly direction behind the spur to the left towards the low col between the summits of Mont Fourchon to the right and Pain de Sucre to the left; occasional signs on the rocks are a help. Near the col you will encounter a scree slope and the path can be difficult to follow; keeping an eye out for worn rocks will help. Follow the path as it trends rightwards just before the col and improves towards the final climb to the summit of **Mont Fourchon (1hr 50min)**.

A simple scramble to the summit ends on the summit blocks (**2hr**). ▶

The return is by the same route and will take about an hour and a quarter.

Pain de Sucre towers over the small pond; time for reflection

Care is needed as there is significant exposure at the summit. The view is as breathtaking as it is far-reaching, Grand Combin and Mont Blanc and its subsidiaries are clearly visible, and the Gran Paradiso range is also visible further south.

ROUTE 25
Two Cols

Start/Finish	Small car park above hairpin bend, approx. 1km down the road from La Cantina, 2075m altitude
Distance	9km
Ascent	620m
Descent	620m
Grade	2 with some technical route finding in descent which requires attention
Time	4hr 10min

This walk has some far-reaching views from the two cols, each with interesting summit structures, including a crucifix honouring local mountain rescue volunteers at Col Crévacol. A lonely valley where ibex and marmots are more likely to be encountered than other walkers is a treasure to behold. The descent is on intermittent and sometimes vague paths, which means more traditional British mountain skills will be required rather than simply following the usual painted markers typical of walks in the Alps.

From the car park follow the farm track via a number of switchbacks to reach the farm buildings at **Praz de Farcoz**, 2229m (**20min**).

Follow the track beneath the buildings and contour the hillside before beginning to climb the path on a rising traverse to cross a stream (or maybe a streambed in the height of summer). ◄ Keep following the path as it steadily climbs. At the summit of the climb be aware that the yellow signposts are at Col d'Arc while our col, **Col de St-Rhémy**, 2550m, (**1hr 15min**), has the *table d'orientation* (orientation table) as its crowning point.

The large mountain bowl to the right is crowned by Mont Fourchon with Pain de Sucre to its right.

From here the path becomes somewhat indistinct for a short time and care is needed to stay on the route. With the orientation table behind you bear left on the path which drops to the ridgeline of glacial moraine a

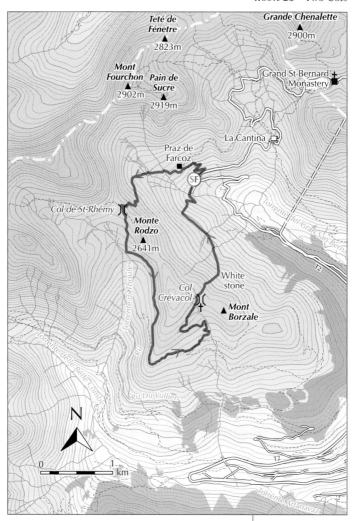

couple of hundred metres away. A small pond makes a
good waypoint marker. Another small pond is the next

Early snow gives the mountains a dusting in late August

This traversing path requires attention as it crosses reasonably steep slopes in the latter part of its route.

waypoint; both are visible from the col. Occasional yellow arrows mark the way. Follow these and the path to reach a rocky defile, 2430m (**1hr 35min**).

This demands care to descend but is soon enough passed. Be careful to take the less obvious path to the left here. It traverses the hillside and can be seen stretching into the distance at the same altitude. Follow this path for approximately 1.5km to reach a **track (2hr 10min)**. ◄

Follow this track as it gently climbs the hillside to a junction (**2hr 30min**).

Take the upper track and within a couple of minutes take the next higher fork and pass a 'white wall' of what looks like limestone (a Path 11A marker is painted here; it is the only time this is seen and it is not marked on

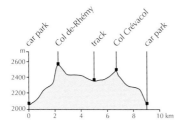

maps). Keep on this path as it zigzags past a small, abandoned building. The old military barracks once used as part of the border controls is visible and, for the energetic, a direct line can be made to this. Before long you will reach the summit of **Col Crévacol**, 2489m (**3hr**).

The remarkable crucifix on Col Crévacol in honour of mountain rescue

The summit has a most interesting and unusual **sculpture** of Christ's Crucifixion. He is crucified on an ice axe with an inscription from Psalm 124: 'Our help is in the name of the Lord who made heaven and earth.' It was placed by the Soccorso Alpino Volontario, the voluntary mountain rescue service in Italy, a partner of the CAI.

The descent from here is potentially tricky as there are numerous paths, many of which peter out. Although the ground is not particularly steep, care is needed and mountain sense will be called upon to pick a route down the blueberry-covered slopes. Two options exist: the first is to traverse on the obvious path left from the summit; this soon peters out leaving you to pick a route down the slopes to a traversing path lower down the hillside. The alternative (and slightly more popular) has a discernible mark on the ground for most of the way and is the recommended descent.

From the summit go directly downhill. After a few metres you will see a faint yellow arrow. Follow the direction of this arrow towards some white, stony ground. Keep descending bearing slightly to the left to avoid steeper rocky ground. Aim towards the now visible motorway tunnel entrance far away. Our waypoint is the darker upright rock. Wend a way to the small shoulder just before the rock. A more distinct path leads to the shoulder, 2370m (**3hr 10min**).

The path now trends leftwards and is clearly visible for a short while. Follow this to a **prominent white stone** (waymarks are painted on this but are faint) (**3hr 15min**).

From this stone the path continues descending leftwards but is less pronounced. The next waypoint is the white rock formation about eight minutes away. Small paths lead towards this and pass below it (**3hr 25min**).

The path improves for a short while to continue descending in a traverse. It is narrow in places, so care is needed.

Pass above two small larch trees on the slope and some alpenrose forming a steep bank. Follow the path to a large, open gully and cross the watercourse (in summer this is likely to be dry) (**3hr 30min**).

Having climbed the other side of the gully, look for a flat piece of greener ground ahead, in line with a hairpin bend on the road. Descend in a shallow traversing line across the slope towards this flatter green feature; there is little in the way of a path but the ground is open and reasonably gentle. On reaching a dry streambed, (**3hr 35min**), descend on the right bank on ever-easier ground to reach a small, level path (**3hr 40min**). ▶

Follow the path left across the green, level piece of ground and over a shoulder. The path is clearly visible but beware of following it too far. After about five minutes, just after some wet ground, you will encounter some white rocks and a barely visible arrow pointing down the streambed. This is the descent path and points towards the road hairpin below. Follow this line downhill, taking care as large sink holes are encountered (but are clearly visible), to join a good track with large rocks lining its sides (**3hr 50min**). Follow this path as it zigzags down the hillside to reach the **stream** close to the road (**4hr 05min**).

Cross the stream, taking care on the stones, and follow the road back to the **car park** (**4hr 10min**).

A key feature to look out for very close to this path is a small man-made water course running along the hillside, visible as a square hole.

ROUTE 26
Grande Chenalette and Pointe de Drône via ferrata

Start/Finish	Great St Bernard Monastery
Distance	6km
Ascent	600m
Descent	600m
Grade	Via ferrata: F to Grande Chenalette; continuation of ridge – mountaineering grade: PD
Time	4hr 55min
Note	Although this route is more of a protected path, some may find the use of via ferrata equipment provides extra reassurance

This real mountain day just tips into the realm of via ferrata. It may be fairer to describe this a protected mountain walk with occasional ladders to overcome any difficulties and a couple of cables to provide reassurance. By continuing along the frontier ridge, which separates Italy and Switzerland, the route becomes something of a beginner's mountaineering expedition. This descent is graded as PD – with grade I/II downclimbing (protected by fixed equipment).

Experienced mountaineers and scramblers will need no specific equipment for this route. Those with less experience or with group members who may need reassurance, a couple of slings and karabiners and a 30m length of confidence rope may well be of use tackling the descent route. Obviously, the mountain skills to belay a member to safety will be a prerequisite.

The access path climbs the hillside in a northerly direction from directly behind the monastery complex, near the museum and kennel entrance. This is an obvious path that gradually becomes less used, as those visitors who are keen to walk a short distance find the mix of altitude and gradient quells their appetite for a mountain walk. We carry on, following occasional red and white

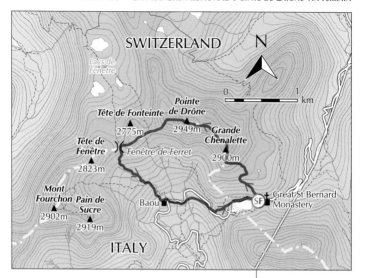

markings, and passing an old cable car station, to the ridgeline and on to Petite Chenalette, 2789m (**1hr**). ▶

The route now takes on a mountain feel. Follow the ridge with slight diversions to small ladders to overcome steep sections. Cables protect exposed but straightforward sections before reaching the flatter summit area

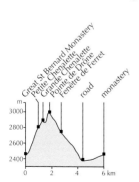

of **Grand Chenalette**, 2889m (**1hr 40min**). Be sure to follow the painted lines here; the path is indistinct. If this feels like enough of a challenge, it is feasible to reverse the route from here in a little over an hour.

Take the ridge as it continues in a north-westerly direction towards a small

The view from here is incredible and includes Gran Paradiso, Mont Blanc and Grand Combin.

177

*The simple ladder
section leading
towards the summit
of Grande Chenalette*

lake (Lac de Fenêtre). The descent along the ridge tips into the realm of mountaineering and as such a rope and some basic belaying equipment might prove useful. The first section is more challenging. Fixed chains and the occasional footplate help on the most difficult sections. This is graded mountaineering grade I/II, so care is certainly required.

After crossing the summit of **Pointe de Drône**, 2949m, (**2hr 40min**), follow the path as it descends with occasional fixed ropes to help you reach **Fenêtre de Ferret**, 2698m (**3hr 25min**).

The hospice is clearly signed via the path to the left; an hour might be optimistic. Follow this as it drops towards the road below. Cross a couple of streams. Beware, in places the path becomes indistinct. Keep an eye out for the worn way and occasional markings. After joining Path 13C, it improves to reach the road at **Baou**, 2389m (**4hr 15min**).

Follow the path to pass beneath the impressive galleried road. Cross the road and take the original Roman road, cut through the rock, to reach the statue of St Bernard, complete with the enchained beasts of the mountains tamed by him to make the crossing safe. The **monastery** is a short walk along the road (**4hr 55min**).

The summit flags and Mont Blanc

UPPER AOSTA VALLEY – COURMAYEUR

Mont Blanc and Val Veny from the summit of Mont de la Saxe (Route 28)

Courmayeur sits nestled among soaring peaks with forests climbing their steep, rocky sides. Its pedestrianised main street hosts a range of shops, restaurants and cafés to meet everyone's needs. A calmer atmosphere than that of Chamonix adds to the ambience of this true mountain town.

A range of hotels and B&Bs serve every budget; the tourist information office is a good starting point (see www.lovevda.it). A particular little gem is Chalet Plan Gorret (www.chaletplangorret.it), a beautiful, small, family-run hotel with six rooms and a fantastic restaurant fusing Sardinian seafood cuisine with the local delicacies. The restaurant is popular with local people (always a very good recommendation in Italy) so book early to avoid disappointment.

The Skyway Monte Bianco is a fabulous construction (and was featured in *Kingsman: The Golden Circle*) and makes for an enjoyable day out with a range of experiences on offer.

A small Alpine museum offers an insight into the pioneers of Alpine mountaineering and allows the handling of artefacts.

There is a popular family walk from the car parks at the head of Val Veny (the exact location of the parking places is season dependent, with the narrow road being closed lower down in the valley in the summer) to Cabane

The viewpoint on Mont Chétif affords wonderful views of the Grand Jorasses and Dent de Géant (Route 32)

du Combal and its small lakeside setting; this will take about an hour to an hour and a half on the road. The more adventurous can continue to Rifugio Elisabetta Soldini, another hour or so up the valley, which offers stunning balcony views as a wonderful lunch spot. Booking is recommended in high season, as this is a very popular destination as well as stopping point on the TMB (+39 165 844080, info@rifugio-elisabetta.com).

Map: 1:25 000 'Carta dei Sentieri' by Escusionista editore 01: Monte Bianco, Courmayeur.

ROUTE 27
Mont Chétif

Start/Finish	Dolonne ski lift car park, Courmayeur
Distance	10.5km
Ascent	1200m full route; 640m from Dolonne top lift; 410m from Col Chécrouit
Descent	1200m full route; 640m from Dolonne top lift; 410m from Col Chécrouit
Grade	2+ for total ascent
Time	5hr 10min for the full route; 3hr from the Dolonne top lift; 2hr 20min approx. from Col Chécrouit chairlift

The pointed summit of Mont Chétif towers over Courmayeur and has a number of interesting routes to reach its summit. The most challenging is the via ferrata (Route 32) but ski lifts can reduce the ascent to a few hundred metres. This route is the real deal as it starts from the mountain's base and climbs every step to the summit. The summit is a long, broad ridge with an impressive 4m statue of the Virgin Mary looking down on Courmayeur. The views of the Mont Blanc range are stunning, while the Matterhorn and Gran Paradiso are visible too.

For those wishing for an easier but still challenging day on the mountain, this route can be started from the top of the bubble lift from Dolonne or by traversing from the chairlift that ends at Col Chécrouit (the chairlift links with the Dolonne lift).

It is not too difficult to imagine the townfolk washing clothes together and sharing the latest news here.

Begin by walking uphill along the road for a couple of hundred metres before taking the sideroad to the right at Hotel Ottoz Meublé, following the markers for the TMB and AV2 (a 2 within a yellow triangle) (**5min**). The route is well marked as it enters the oldest part of the town and wends its way through passageways too narrow for cars. Turn left at the end of the first small road, then bear right at a church to pass the ancient laundry washing basins (**10min**). ◄

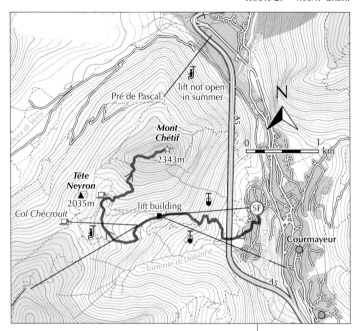

Carry on up the road to go underneath a prominent 'Fun Park' sign across the road. Take the path which is signed off this road to the right a couple of hundred metres further on (**15min**).

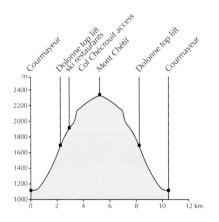

Follow this path as it enters the woodland and begins a steady climb that becomes a series of zigzags to join a sharp hairpin bend of the ski access road (**40min**).

Continue on the path as it re-enters the woodland.

183

A short level section offers views down to the valley far below (**55min**). The Dolonne ski lift station is soon within sight. Continue along the path which climbs more steeply beneath the **lift infrastructure** to reach the station, 1710m (**1hr 10min**).

The path climbs through the ski domain and may be redirected due to summer works being undertaken. Essentially, follow the path to the left of the ski area as you're looking uphill (towards the restaurant Les Dames Anglais). Follow yellow painted posts across the hillside to reach the large vehicle access track (**1hr 25min**). Cross the track, still following the TMB signs, and climb to the left to reach the ski restaurants a few hundred metres to the right of the Col Chécrouit upper ski lift (**1hr 35min**).

Approaching the summit of Mont Chétif with Mont Blanc behind

This is the point at which those from the Col Chécrouit ski lift join the route, about 10 minutes' walk along the tracks from the top lift station.

Mont Chétif is signed here on Path 5 (within a couple of minutes it is signed as 5A; no matter, it is the Mont Chétif path). Follow the path into the shaded woodland and, before long, the first views of the Mont Blanc massif emerge from between the trees. Keep following the path to reach a **junction**, 2125m (**2hr 05min**). Do not take Path 5, which descends to Pré de Pascal. From this junction keep ascending on the well-worn path to reach the base of a short but steep and narrow gully. Clamber up this to reach a surprisingly narrow col (**2hr 20min**).

Follow the path to the right along a welcome level section to the bottom of a wide, dry valley (**2hr 25min**). Beware, a path continues into this valley but the correct route is to the right. Follow the path to the right to reach a junction with Path 4, 2245m (**2hr 30min**).

Climb the steeper ground ahead in a series of zigzags to arrive at the summit ridge of **Mont Chétif**, 2343m (**2hr 55min**). Five minutes further along is the statue of the Virgin Mary and a real bird's eye view of Courmayeur.

The return is by the same path. Care is required on the descent as there are loose stones and awkward ground to manage. The steep gully is reached in 25 minutes ((**3hr 20min**)), the ski restaurants in 50 minutes ((**3hr 45min**)), the upper Dolonne ski station in 1 hour and 15 minutes ((**4hr 10min**)) and the centre of **Courmayeur** in approximately 2 hours and 15 minutes (**5hr 10min**).

The Madonna looking down on Courmayeur and Val Ferret

ROUTE 28

Mont de la Saxe and Col Sapin

Start/Finish	Car park at Villair, Courmayeur
Distance	12km
Ascent	1100m
Descent	1100m
Grade	2
Time	6hr 30min

The views from the whale-back ridge forming the summit of Mont de la Saxe are some of the best in this part of the Alps. The multitude of summits, glaciers and rocky ridges across Val Ferret continually draw your attention. Binoculars are a must to allow you to identify the mountain huts perched on outcrops on the Mont Blanc range. The aptly named Dent du Géant (Giant's Tooth) should be easy to spot. With a bit of luck, it will be possible to see the Col de la Seigne and, therefore, the border with Italy and, in the opposite direction, the Col du Grand Ferret, the border with Switzerland.

The water management 'waterfalls' here are both interesting and, after recent rainfall, picturesque.

The route is likely to be quite popular as it is the TMB 'main road' out of Courmayeur.

It is possible to walk from the centre of Courmayeur to the start but this is only worthwhile if staying in the centre of the town.

From the car park at the end of the road take the track as it climbs up the valley for about 100 metres before taking a left turn over the river on a bridge. ◄ Follow Path 42 (also the TMB) and signs for Rifugio Bertoni. ◄ Pass the memorial to the Aosta Battalion, **(25min)**, and continue upwards to break the treeline at about 1800m **(1hr)**.

The **memorial** commemorates the Aosta Battalion, an elite group of soldiers with specific mountain skills. During World War 1 the battalion was awarded the MOVM, Gold Medal of Military Valour, in recognition of their actions on Monte Solarolo in which 23 of the 25 officers and 773 of the 800

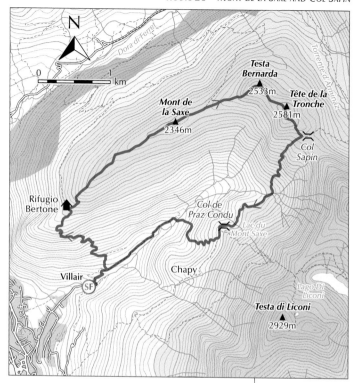

troops were injured or killed repelling the invading Austrian forces in the Veneto region of Italy.

Follow the path as it rounds a corner. The first real views of Mont Blanc will make most want to pause, catch a breath and take in the view. Keep following the path to reach **Rifugio Bertone**, 1977m (**1hr 30min**). ▸

It will be hard to resist a coffee break here; the view alone is worthy of a stop!

From the refuge continue on Path 42 to reach the small orientation table, 2045m (**1hr 40min**). From here things get quieter as most trekkers will bear left on the TMB. Our path continues up the broad ridgeline, passing the avalanche protection fences. The gradient eases

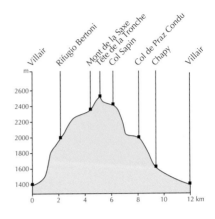

off and the views just get better and better. Keep follow-ing the path to reach **Lac du Mont Saxe**, 2346m, (**2hr 30min**), where, with still water, the mountains reflect per-fectly in the water. After you have passed over the nearby summit of Mont de la Saxe, the summit of Testa Bernarda

The memorial to the Aosta Battalion

is the next objective and will be clearly visible 1.5km along the ridge. Keep following the path until, at approximately 2425m, a smaller path diverges towards the small summit cairn. **Testa Bernarda**, 2533m (**3hr 15min**). ▸

It is possible to bypass this summit on the 'main path' but the views make the effort worthwhile.

The next summit is not too far away, after a short descent to the main path climb to the summit of **Tête de la Tronche**, 2581m (**3hr 35min**). The descent requires care but before long you will reach **Col Sapin** (Colle Sapine), 2435m (**3hr 55min**).

From the col the path can be spotted wending its way across the mountainside ahead. It is worth spotting the chalets of Curru from here; this is the next objective. Follow Path 43 rightwards from the col down an initially steep slope to cross the **stream** and make a short ascent passing Curru to **Col de Praz Condu**. From here drop to the path junction, 1957m (**5hr**).

Take Path 43 route directly downhill (steep at first) to Chapy, (**5hr 40min**), (Tsapy on the map) and then down the valley on a track to return to the **car park** (**6hr 30min**).

Reflection of the Grandes Jorasses in Lac du Mont Saxe

ROUTE 29
Rifugio Bonatti and Mont Blanc panorama

Start/Finish	Lavachey car park/bus stop
Distance	6km/11km
Ascent	390m/540m
Descent	390m/950m
Grade	2
Time	2hr 35min, 2hr 50min or 4hr 55min, depending on option taken

With two options, this walk can be a morning or afternoon excursion with a refuge lunch included, or it can be more of a day's walk by following the TMB/AV1 (Giants' Trail) to Courmayeur.

There is no more famous mountaineer in Italy than Walter Bonatti; a visit to the refuge named after him is almost a pilgrimage. The crowds of trekkers at the refuge may be a surprise but the views of the Mont Blanc massif more than make up for the crowds.

The TMB is probably the most famous long-distance trek in the world and the option to complete a section of the trail exists here. The reasonably short, and mainly downhill, section from Rifugio Bonatti to Courmayeur offers superlative views of the Italian side of Mont Blanc.

The Green Line bus is the shuttle bus into Val Ferret, a regular service departing from the bus station at the lower end of the town. In the summer season it departs every 15 to 30 minutes depending on the time of day.

Val Ferret is a busy valley with plenty of car parks. In high season the local council blocks the road at certain points to ease congestion in the upper valley. A cheap bus service runs from Courmayeur, and shuttle buses run at regular periods along the valley; these can be used to reduce any road-walking sections or to simplify logistics for the longer traverse.

Due to melting of the glaciers high on Mont Blanc, the road and all access to Val Ferret have been closed for short periods when ice falls and there is a high risk of landslides.

From one of the car parks (or bus stop) at Lavachey follow the road for a few metres before taking a small path

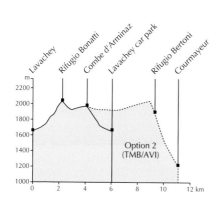

WALTER BONATTI, 1930–2011

Bonatti pioneered many routes which even today make for demanding expeditions. He was a proponent of 'pure' climbing and was against the use of technical support, such as bolts.

For many years, following the 1954 expedition to K2, Bonatti was wrongly accused of making decisions that caused Amir Mehdi, a Hunza climber from Pakistan, to lose his toes to frostbite. It wasn't until 2007 that the CAI finally published a truthful account of the events, which exonerated Bonatti of any wrongdoing. It was after this expedition that Bonatti settled in Courmayeur as a mountain guide.

He climbed extensively on the mountains facing the refuge named after him. The Grandes Jorasses has many pinnacled summits, one of which is named after Edward Whymper, the first to climb the Matterhorn. The 1100m Bonatti–Vaucher route is still considered a formidable undertaking today.

His last route as a professional was the first winter ascent of the north face of the Matterhorn (Nordwand) in 1965, a significant achievement, particularly as it was a solo climb. After this he continued to explore every corner of the earth, including undertaking expeditions along the Amazon and Orinoco Rivers, studying tigers in Sumatra and exploring Central Australia and the Patagonian ice fields. Images of some of these expeditions can be found on the walls of the refuge built in his honour in 1998.

The refuge offers refreshments all day along with more substantial meals at lunchtime. It is a very busy place with trekkers passing throughout the day.

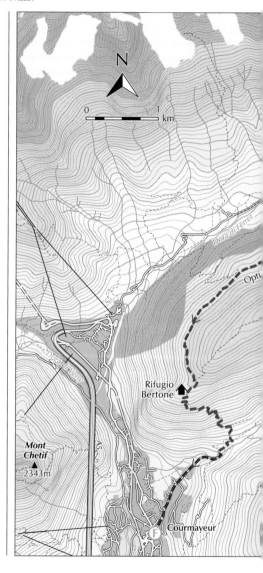

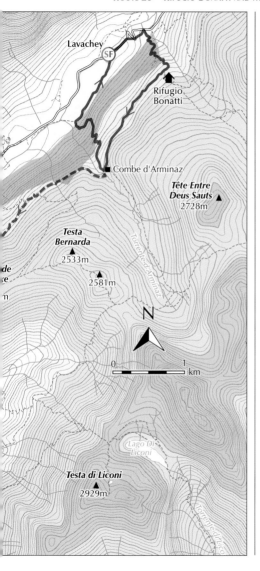

Gaining the tree line with the Mont Blanc massif behind

which leaves the road at the first bend in the road to short cut to a track (or follow the tarmac road to the road–track junction just before the river and then leave the road on the track). Whichever of these two starts you choose, the track climbs uphill via numerous zigzags. Keep on this track to reach a signpost for Path 28 and 42 at 1855m **(25min)**.

You will probably encounter runners training for the UTMB as well as intrepid mountain bikers. The trail is likely to be busy and a share-and-share-alike attitude is important, as there is no distinct right-of-way legislation.

Continue climbing the hillside taking time to enjoy the ever-improving views of Mont Blanc and, closer, Les Grandes Jorasses until you reach the treeline and another path junction **(45min)**. Rifugio Bonatti is signposted as five minutes from here; there are also markers for both the TMB and AV1. The five minutes may be a little optimistic, although the refuge will be within reach in less than ten. **Rifugio Bonatti** (2025m) **(55min)**. ◀

Option 1: A descent to Val Ferret: 1hr 40min from Rifugio Bonatti

From the refuge descend left towards the enormous bulk of Mont Blanc. The path levels to pass above the alpage

of Sécheron before climbing to a path junction at the opening of **Combe d'Arminaz** (1hr 40min).

Take Path 29, which descends to pass through the farm buildings above the stream. Keep following the path

The view from Rifugio Bonatti, a fitting celebration of a mountain legend

as it traverses the hillside and begin a series of zigzags to lose height quickly. Continue descending and as the path becomes rockier and eroded, leave the tree cover in the base of the valley (**2hr 30min**).

Take the path either leftwards to join the road close to the bus stop at Praz Sec (Prasec on the bus map), (**2hr 35min**), or rightwards to **Lavachey** and the car park (**2hr 50min**).

Option 2: The TMB/AV1 traverse: 4hr from Rifugio Bonatti to Courmayeur

If this is the preferred option, take a shuttle bus from Courmayeur to the start.

From the refuge descend leftwards to pass above the alpage of Sécheron before gently climbing to a corner and enter the side valley of **Combe d'Arminaz**. Ignore the descending vague path below and the follow the main path to join Path 29 (**1hr 40min**).

Cross the wooden bridge and climb out of the combe to follow a well-worn section of path. After the **junction** with Path 30 there is a small pond that offers wonderful reflections of Mont Blanc (**2hr 30min**).

Pass Alpe Lenchey and gently climb to arrive at an orientation table at 2055m and a path junction (**3hr 15min**).

Descend to **Rifugio Bertone** (**3hr 25min**).

Begin a series of zigzags to descend into Val Sapin passing a military memorial on the way to join a track which can be followed, although small paths cut some of the corners.

The track gradually becomes a road. Keep descending, passing a memorial to the mountain guides of Courmayeur before suddenly popping out into the heart of the village at the Società delle Guide Alpine, a small museum and information centre (**4hr 55min**).

ROUTE 30
Mont Fortin

Start/Finish	Chalet del Miage (car park or bus stop)
Distance	19.5km
Ascent	1250m
Descent	1250m
Grade	3
Time	6hr 25min

A favourite with locals and something of a hidden treasure, this summit offers fabulous views of Mont Blanc. The old military buildings on the summit remind walkers of the turbulent past of those regions on international borders. A number of refuges offer refreshment opportunities on the descent, and a regular bus service means this route can be accessed from Courmayeur without the need to drive.

Some exposed ground near the summit, the significant ascent and the length of the route make this route a grade 3.

From the car park take the road beyond the 'route bar-rée' sign that blocks the road to traffic. In summer the road may well be closed lower down the valley to mini-mise congestion; in which case, park in the obligatory car park and follow the closed road to Chalet del Miage (about 20 minutes additional walking). The bus will always go to Chalet del Miage, a popular restaurant and café stop.

Follow the road until just before Cabane du Combal, reaching a bridge, **Pont Combal** 1954m (**1hr 10min**).

Cross the bridge and then take the well-signed Path 9 to the left and uphill, approximately 150 metres from the bridge. ▶ At approximately **2225m the path splits**; the TMB continues straight on but we take the right-hand fork, Path 9 ▶ (**1hr 45min**).

The path may be busy as it is part of the TMB. It offers ever-improving views of Mont Blanc, Les Grandes Jorasses, the obvious needle of Aiguille Noire de Peuterey and Val Ferret.

Standing stones with path numbers identify the two options.

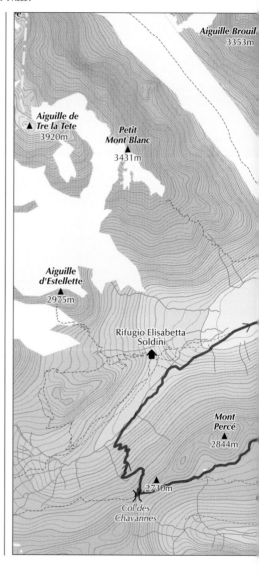

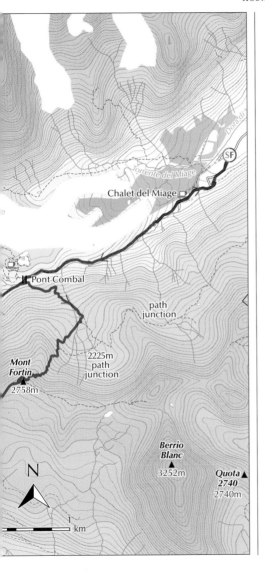

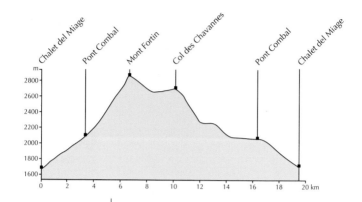

Follow this narrower path across level ground and after a few hundred metres begin climbing the hillside in a series of zigzags. The path becomes less distinct as the vegetation gives way to rockier terrain, but cairns help to identify the path in the upper reaches. At approximately 2650m the path bears rightwards to begin a long loop, avoiding the more difficult terrain directly ahead. After traversing along an exposed path under the summit you reach a path junction. Take the path left and uphill to the summit of **Mont Fortin**, 2758m (**3hr 25min**).

An **orientation table** helps to identify the summits in sight, and what a range there is: Monte Rosa, Matterhorn (Cervin), Grandes Jorasses, Gran Paradiso, Gran Combin and, of course, Mont Blanc.

On the summit there are the remains of **military troop shelters** from before World War 2, when continuing tensions meant these high valleys were under constant observation. The highest battle of World War 2 took place on the slopes of Mont Blanc when troops from Nazi-controlled Courmayeur attempted to take the summit. The conflict lasted from October 1944 until February 1945, when Free French troops, with British support, secretly

brought cannons up from Chamonix and shelled German mountain troops in the Fréty refuge (now the Pavilion on the Skyway).

Looking down Val Veny and over to the Mont Blanc massif

The next objective is Col des Chavannes, a couple of kilometres up the valley. From the summit take Path 10 towards the small lakes below the impressive summit of Mont Percé. This pleasant path meanders along this high plateau with eagles above and whistling marmots below. At the **Col des Chavannes** (col of the goats), **(4hr 15min)**, take the initially steep descending Path 11 (more clearly marked as AV2: a 2 inside a triangle) rightwards into the upper reaches of Val Veny. The path resumes a gentler gradient to reach the bottom of the valley **(4hr 55min)**.

Lower Val Veny near Chalet del Miage

Follow the path along the flat valley bottom to reach a wooden bridge (**5hr 10min**).

This bridge can be crossed to reach Rifugio Elisabetta Soldini in about 10 minutes. Alternatively, continue along the path ahead which stays on the right bank of the river or, if your knees are protesting, stay on the vehicle track. The path joins the track to Pont Combal, 1954m (**5hr 55min**).

Follow the familiar track back to **Chalet del Miage** for some well-earned refreshments; this will take about half an hour (**6hr 25min**).

ROUTE 31
Tour of the Pyramides Calcaires

Start/Finish	Car parks at the Chalet del Miage – these vary according to the time of year. In high season they may be further down the valley, adding half an hour to the approach and another 20 minutes to the return. Those staying at the Hobo campsite can access this high point via their shuttle bus.
Distance	19km
Ascent	950m
Descent	950m
Grade	2
Time	5hr 30min

While almost within sight of the famous TMB, this less visited corner will reward the intrepid walker with hidden gems in the form of World War 2 battle remains and, probably, close encounters with wildlife rarely seen on the busy, noisy TMB path less than a kilometre away. This quiet corner has the feel of being high in the mountains and provides a rare moment of peace away from the crowds.

Begin by following the road from the car park and, later on, a track to **Pont Combal**, 1954m **(50min)**. ▶

Cross the bridge and continue along the track towards Rifugio Elisabetta Soldini. There is what appears to be a short cut to the left. In reality, this saves little if any time and rejoins the track. Whichever of the two you choose, the final track arrives at the door of **Rifugio Elisabetta Soldini**, 2197m **(1hr 50min)**. ▶

The route continues behind the refuge on Path 12 (the most recent maps indicate Path 13 but no markings will be found). The path is reasonably worn and well marked as it climbs the ridge. After around 15 minutes of ascent a worn path leaves Path 12 and enters the narrow valley,

The views of the Pyramides from the road will be an inspiring focus with the Col des Pyramides Calcaires clearly visible.

The refuge has a fabulous terrace offering views down the valley and to the summits above.

The jagged teeth of Pyramides Calcaires in the distance

which often holds snow late into the summer. Either path can be taken but it is worth noting that the valley path is indistinct. The route is reasonably obvious. Climb the

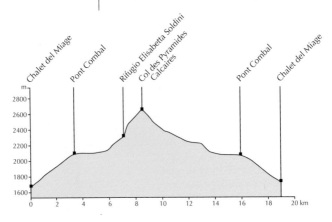

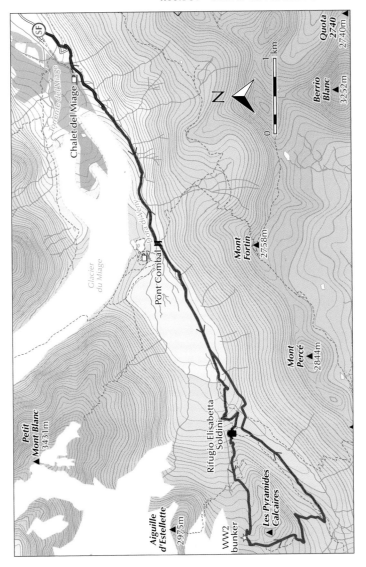

Leaving Rifugio Elisabetta Soldini and Val Veny

The small military installation above the col is worthy of investigation by those interested in military history and appears to have been thoroughly destroyed.

length of the small valley and ascend the 'headwall' to rejoin Path 12 as it traverses leftwards towards the **Col des Pyramides Calcaires**, 2573m (**3hr 10min**). ◄

This was one of the highest battle sites in **World War 2**. Hitler was determined to occupy the summit of Mont Blanc in the winter of 1944–1945. This region was occupied by Nazi forces supported by Fascist Italians and saw fighting between allied mountain troops from Chamonix and opposing forces across the Vallée Blanche at an altitude of over 3000m, in winter conditions.

The opposing troops were stationed in mountain huts, some of which were destroyed by enemy fire. Slit trenches cut into the glacier provided defensive positions, as well as more substantial blockhouses lower down the mountainsides. Another of these can be seen later in the walk.

Having explored the military remains, and maybe been lucky enough to observe the *bouquetins* (known as steinbock in Italian or ibex elsewhere) that often congregate in this quiet corner, continue following the path over the summit of the col. ▸

In the distance the Col de la Seigne is visible: the border between Italy and France and one of the main passes on the TMB.

The descent twists and turns as it passes mounds of discarded barbed wire, another symbol of previous hostilities in these high places. Before long join the large, eroded path of the TMB at a wooden bridge, 2290m (**3hr 50min**).

Follow the TMB down the valley to arrive at the access **path junction** for the Rifugio Elisabetta Soldini, 2145m (**4hr 15min**). The eagle-eyed will notice small observation posts and military emplacements in the cliffs above the path along this section.

The route now follows the outward track. Either the shorter, more direct path or the gentler, longer track can be taken to reach the Combal plain below and on to the bridge, 1954m (**5hr**). ▸ Follow the road to the **car park**, 1700m (**5hr 30min**).

There is the option to divert to the Cabane du Combal for refreshments.

ROUTE 32
Mont Chétif via ferrata

Start	Car park, Courmayeur Sports Centre, Villette, less than a 10min walk from the town centre
Finish	Dolonne ski lift station
Distance	6km to lift station
Ascent	1200m
Descent	600m
Grade	F
Time	6hr 25min
Note	The first section of this route involves a via ferrata for which specialised equipment (see box below) and prior experience is required

Although this is a comparatively easy via ferrata, with around 1200m of ascent this route is a full mountain day. Exposed ledges and open faces are traversed and ascended early on to climb above Courmayeur, which looks like a model village below. Once you have passed the via ferrata section, a rocky, narrow path traverses the mountain; rock climbers also use this as an access path to the many routes on the cliffs near the summit of Mont Chétif. The view from the summit is ample reward for the effort required to attain this lofty peak. It takes in many Alpine giants, including the nearby Mont Blanc, so don't forget the binoculars! As the summit is visible from the centre of Courmayeur, a summiteer can wave to friends or family enjoying the delights of the town.

Although technically simple, this route demands correct via ferrata equipment: a harness and via ferrata self belay system are essential, as is a helmet – if for no reason that to protect you from dislodged rocks from people above you. Gloves are recommended as the chains and cables can have sharp edges.

Finding the start of the via ferrata is a little tricky as the path is one of many locals' paths twisting through the woodland to reach the bottom of the cliffs.

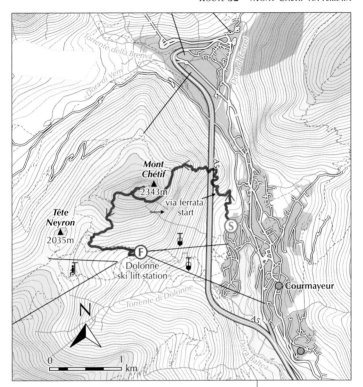

From the sports centre Path 4 is clearly marked across fields but doesn't mention any via ferrata. Follow the well-worn path into woodland. From here it is confusing due to lots of mountain-bike trails and no waymarking of the path. Keep towards the right, this path looks more 'path-like' than others, to reach a junction with a signpost that indicates Path 4. Follow this leftwards and the bottom of the cliff comes into view between trees. Follow the path to the bottom of the cliff (some easy beginner rock climbing here) (**20min**).

Follow the path leftwards at the cliff base. The signs indicate a via ferrata now. At approximately

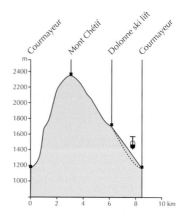

Courmayeur   Mont Chétif   Dolonne ski lift   Courmayeur

The views down to Courmayeur are worth stopping for here.

1450m the first chains will be found (**40min**). Clip into these as you would a cable. Traverse across the rock in sunshine gaining height to reach a step across a small gap and follow the cable then chain in a gently rising traverse. ◀

Traversing Mont Chétif above Courmayeur

Follow the chains which continue onto easier ground with short, unprotected but simple sections. On the sections without chains, yellow paint marking indicates the route. A viewpoint with wooden fencing makes for a good point to have a break and admire the new view towards the Mont Blanc range. The Dent du Géant is the obvious square rock pinnacle, with Grand Jorasses to the right (**1hr 25min**).

Clip into the short chain sections, which protect simple scramble sections, to gain height and enter forest cover and, eventually, you will arrive at a **path junction**, 1995m (**2hr 25min**).

At the junction take the path leftwards, still Path 4. This quickly becomes a narrow path which rises and falls as it traverses the open, rocky mountainside. ▶

Before a huge gully with a large square communications reflector sited above it, take the path which climbs rightwards before the gully, this climbs steeply to reach an open valley above the reflector (**3hr**).

Follow the yellow-marked path leftwards to join a path junction (**3hr 20min**). ▶

From the junction take Path 5 rightwards, signed for Mont Chétif. This is a steep path which is loose in places; care is advised.

Climb the final 100m to reach the summit. **Mont Chétif**, 2343m (**3hr 45min**).

The statue, about 4m in height, of the **Virgin Mary** stands a short distance away and gives a commanding view of Courmayeur. This statue is visible from Courmayeur too, so it is feasible to arrange for a photograph of successful summiteers!

Topo Chetif VF

Climbers will be encountered on the path as they gear up for the routes above.

The views of Mont Blanc here are impressive and it can be a busy spot as Path 5 is accessible from the nearby ski lift which operates in the summer.

The Madonna looking down on Courmayeur and Val Ferret

Descend by the same path which demands care in descent. At the junction of paths encountered earlier take Path 5. Follow this along a pleasant level section before beginning another steep, attention-demanding section.

At another path junction, **(4hr 05min)**, which is less clearly marked but has signs to Dolonne (the ski lift top station), take the path towards the restaurants which continues to drop steadily through mixed forests to reach the ski station buildings. The refuge and café are to the right and clearly seen on leaving the forest line **(4hr 30min)**.

Take the track to the refuge, **(4hr 35min)**, to enjoy a well-earned drink. Alternatively, take one of the myriad of paths which drop to join the large vehicle access track clearly visible below. This section is often under redevelopment in the summer so paths change according to ground works being undertaken. The **cable car station** is reached and will offer a quick, knee-saving descent to Courmayeur (**4hr 55min**). The one on the left is a bubble lift that serves Dolonne and arrives close to the sports station in Courmayeur. The large gondola to the right serves the southern end of Courmayeur.

It is also possible to walk along the TMB trail into **Courmayeur**, should the decent so far be insufficient for your legs! This involves a 600m descent in a couple of kilometres and will take around an hour and a half.

APPENDIX A
Useful contacts

Transport
TrekBus
tel +39 166 940986

Arriva Italia (buses
)https://aosta.arriva.it

SVAP (buses)
www.svap.it

Tourist offices
www.lovevda.it

Donnas (Main valley)
tel +39 125 804843
vallecentrale@turismo,vda,it

Gressoney-Saint-Jean
tel +39 125 355185
gressoneysaintjean@turismo.vda.it

Breuil-Cervinia
tel +39 166 949136
cervinia@turismo.vda.it

Aosta
tel +39 165 236627
aosta@turismo.vda.it

Valpelline
tel +39 333 6163329
aosta@turismo.vda.it

Courmayeur
tel +39 165 842060
aosta@turismo.vda.it

Accommodation and mountain refuges
Links to accommodation throughout the Aosta Valley can be found at
www.aosta-valley.co.uk

Lys valley
Etoile du Berger
hotel, twin and double rooms
tel +39 340 5206774
www.letoileduberger.it

Rifugio Barma
independent, sleeps 54
tel +39 331 1087009
rifugiobarma@gmail.com
www.rifugiobarma.it

La Gruba Hotel
private hotel, 10 rooms
tel +39 340 8270110
www.lagrubarelais.com

Valtournenche/Cervinia
Rifugio Barmasse
sleeps 25, private
tel +39 345 1081551
www.rifugiocuney.it/it/
il-rifugio-barmasse

Camping Glair
Shaded pitches, laundry facilities, Wi-Fi,
restaurant within walking distance.
tel +39 166 92077
info@campingglair.it
www.campingglair.it

Valpelline
Hotel Valentino
12 rooms, half board available
tel +39 165 730901
www.hotelvalentinobionaz.com

Clé du Paradis B&B
restaurants in nearby Lexert, 6 rooms
tel +39 165 730016
www.cleduparadis.it

La Tour – Food, Bed & Trekking,
Oyacedortoir accommodation option,
restaurant on site
tel +39 165 730119
valle-daosta-hotels.com

Rifugio Champillon
private, 30 beds
tel +39 320 225 3348 or +39 339 6359
679
rifugiochampillon@gmail.com
www.rifugio-champillon.it

Camping Grand Combin
Shaded pitches, swimming pool,
laundry facilities, shop, café/restaurant
tel +39 165 73250
info@grandcombin.com
www.grandcombin.com

Camping Lexert
Laundry facilities, restaurant, bar and
shop on site
tel +39 165 730109
info@campinglaclexert.it
www.campinglaclexert.it

Great St Bernard Pass
Great St Bernard Monastery
tel +41 27 787 12 36
hospice@gsbernard.com
www.gsbernard.com

Great St Bernard Auberge (Hotel)
tel +41 27 787 11 53
info@aubergehospice.ch
www.aubergehospice.ch

Rifugio Frassati
64 beds private (charitable trust)
tel + 39 331 943 8054
info@rifugiofrassati.it

Courmayeur
There is no campsite close to
Courmayeur, but the following
campsites are located a couple of
kilometres up the valley:

Val Veny
Camping Aiguille Noire
tel +39 347 547 7941
www.aiguillenoire.com

Hobo Camping
tel +39 165 869073
www.campinghobo.com

Camping Monte Bianco la Sorgenti
tel: +39 389 902 0772
www.campinglasorgente.net

Camping Val Veny Cuignon
tel +39 165 869073
www.grandesjorasses.com

Rifugio Bonatti
private, 78 beds
tel +39 165 1855523
www.rifugiobonatti.it

Val Ferret
Camping Grand Jorasses
tel: +39 165 869708
www.grandjorasses.com

Camping Tronchey
tel: +39 165 89193
www.tronchey.com

Rifugio Elisabetta Soldini
CAI, 72 beds
tel +39 165 844080
info@rifugioelisabetta.com

Mapping
Stanfords (maps and guidebooks for travelling):
www.stanfords.co.uk
Escursionista (available from Stanfords):
www.escursionistaeditore.com
Swiss Topo (includes app): www.swisstopo.ch

Weather
YR (includes app): www.yr.no/?spr=eng

Miscellaneous
'The world of Alpine flowersie' – app (identifies Alpine flowers)

APPENDIX B

Useful phrases

The Aosta valley is a multilingual area. French is often spoken as capably as Italian. English tends to be spoken less frequently (more so in the tourist hotspots). A well-intentioned attempt in either Italian or French will be welcomed.

Pleasantries and manners

English	Italian	French
thank you	grazie	merci
please	per favore	s'il vous plaît
hello, good day	buon giorno	bonjour
good evening/goodnight	buona sera	bonsoir
goodbye	arrivederci	au revoir
less formal greeting 'hi'	salve	salut

Navigation/route finding

English	Italian	French
left	sinistra	gauche
right	destra	droite
ahead	avanti	tout droit
map	carta	carte
compass	bussola	boussole
guidebook	guida	guide
route	itinerario	parcours
north	nord	nord
south	sud	sud
east	est	est

English	Italian	French
west	ovest	ouest
stage/leg (in a walk)	tappe	étape
path (a footpath)	sentiero	sentier
track (off-road vehicle track)	carreg-giabile	chemin
road	strada	route
ridge	creta	crête
pass	colle	col
glacier	glacier	glacier
summit	vetta	sommet
tarn, small lake	lac/lago	lac
junction	incrocio	jonction
stream	corrente	ruisseau
river	fiume	rivière
wood	bosco	bois
rock	rocce	rocher
dam	diga	barrage
bridge	ponte	pont

Accommodation

English	Italian	French
mountain hut	rifugio	refuge
half board	mezza pensione	demi-pension
dormitory	dormitorio	dortoir
tent	tenda	tente
campsite	area di campeggio	camping

Numbers

English	Italian	French
zero	zero	zéro
one	uno	un
two	due	deux
three	tre	trois
four	quattro	quatre
five	cinque	cinq
six	sei	six
seven	sette	sept
eight	otto	huit
nine	nove	neuf
ten	diece	dix
eleven	undici	onze
twelve	dodici	douze
thirteen	tredici	treize
fourteen	quattrodici	quatorze
fifteen	quidici	quinze
sixteen	sedici	seize
seventeen	diciassette	dix-sept

English	Italian	French
eighteen	diciotto	dix-huit
nineteen	diciannove	dix-neuf
twenty	venti	vingt
thirty	trenta	trente
forty	quaranta	quarante
fifty	cinquanta	cinquante
sixty	sessanta	soixante
seventy	settanta	soixante-dix
eighty	ottanta	quatre-vingt
ninety	novanta	quatre-vingt-dix
one hundred	cento	cent

Days

English	Italian	French
today	oggi	aujourd'hui
tomorrow	domani	demain
yesterday	ieri	hier
Monday	lunedì	lundi
Tuesday	martedì	mardi
Wednesday	mercoledì	mercredi
Thursday	giovedì	jeudi
Friday	venerdì	vendredi
Saturday	sabato	samedi
Sunday	domenica	dimanche

Weather

English	Italian	French
weather forecast	previsioni	météo

APPENDIX B – USEFUL PHRASES

English	Italian	French
snow	neve	neige
fog	nebbia	brouillard
storm (thundery)	tempesta	orage (orageux)
rain	pioggia	pluie
wind	vento	vent
sunny	sole	ensoleillé
cold	freddo	froid
hot	caldo	chaud
ice	ghiaccio	glace

Useful phrases

English (E): I would like to reserve…
dormitory places for tonight, please
Italian (I): Mi piacerebbe prenotare…
posti dormitorio stanotte, per favore
French (F): Je voudrais réserver…lits
pour cette nuit, s'il vous plaît

E: I would like to reserve…dormitory
places for tomorrow night, please

I: Mi piacerebbe prenotare…i dormitori
domani sera, per favore

F: Je voudrais réserver…lits pour demain
soir, s'il vous plaît

E: I would like half board

I: Vorrei la mezza pensione

F: Je voudrais la demi-pension, s'il vous
plaît

E: I would like to buy…packed lunches
please
I: Vorrei comprare…pranzi al sacco,
per favore

F: Je voudrais acheter…pique-niques,
s'il vous plaît

E: We will arrive…
I: Arriveremo…
F: Nous arriverons à…

Accidents and emergencies
E: I have had an accident at…
I: Ho avuto un incidente a…
F: J'ai eu un accident à…

E: My GPS location is…
I: La mia posizione GPS è…
F: Ma position GPS est…

E: We have…casualties
I: Abbiamo…vittime
F: Nous avons…blessés

E: He/she has injured his/her leg/head/
back/arm
I: Lui/lei ha ferito il suo/lei gamba/testa/
schiena/braccio
F: Il/Elle s'est blessé/e à la jambe/tête/
dos/bras

E: We need a helicopter
I: Abbiamo bisogno di un elicottero
F: Nous avons besoin d'un hélicoptère

E: We need an ambulance
I: Abbiamo bisogno di un'ambulanza
F: Nous avons besoin d'une ambulance

E: We need help
I: Abbiamo bisogno di aiuto
F: Nous avons besoin d'aide

APPENDIX C
Clothing and equipment

Mountain weather can be unpredictable and, when stormy weather comes in, it can turn very quickly. Even in the most settled of weather it is foolhardy to leave home without the essentials required to look after yourselves should the weather turn or you have an accident.

Note: Identification should be carried at all times in Italy; a driver's licence or passport will suffice.

- Rucksack: a 20–30 litre capacity rucksack should be large enough to contain everything required for a day walk with space to spare. Good back ventilation and pockets will be valued on the trail
- Boots or walking shoes: worn-in boots that are stiff enough to resist rocky paths but flexible enough to be comfortable for long days on the trail. Trainers can be uncomfortable on rocky paths; walking shoes offer more comfort on rocky ground
- Socks: a thin liner sock and thicker walking sock are a good combination to battle blisters
- Zip-off trekking trousers: these allow 'conversion' to shorts when the temperature rises; conversely, they allow shorts to be turned into trousers if the temperature drops
- T-shirt: a wicking T-shirt makes things much more comfortable
- Midlayer: a fleece or two will be appreciated in the higher mountains
- Waterproof outer layer, including overtrousers
- Light gloves and warm hat or buff
- Sun hat with substantial brim
- Suncream: factor 30 or higher is recommended as the sun can be very strong at altitude
- Good-quality sunglasses of a wrap-around style to keep out glare, the sun is much stronger at altitude
- Trekking poles: a personal choice but very useful for long ascents and descents

Overnight hut kit
Should you spend a night in one of the refuges, you will require the following:

- Sleep wear (or use the 'spare' top)
- Sheet sleeping bag: these are obligatory (one-use ones can be bought at most huts)
- Ear plugs: essential for busy dormitories!
- Wash kit and towel: many refuges now have showers
- A good book or reading device
- Personal medication

- Small headtorch for the dormitory

Group equipment

- A small first-aid kit, including blister kit
- Maps, compass, guidebook
- Phrasebook
- Camera
- Phone (save battery life by keeping offline during the day)
- A bothy bag or some form of emergency shelter, such as a survival bag
- A small pair of binoculars can be very useful for spotting

Via Ferrata

Via ferrata equipment is essential for Route 32. It should also be carried for Route 26.

- Helmet
- Climbing harness
- Specific via ferrata self-belay device
- Gloves – highly recommended
- Stiff footwear – rungs can get painful in training shoes
- A short length of rope to belay less confident members of a group (and always children)
- A rucksack with drinks, snacks and additional clothing

Trail running

While the temptation to go light and fast is strong, it is worth remembering that snow can fall at 2000m+ any time of year and you need to be dressed accordingly.

The 'train hard, race light' maxim works well – carrying a little more kit to keep you safe will help make the race somewhat easier. Also, it is worth remembering that race 'minimum kit' lists are compiled with race marshalling in place. When training, this back up will not be there.

The kit list for the 114km Monte Rosa Walser race is as follows:

- Backpack/vest to carry equipment
- Water container/bladder
- Drinking cup (for feed stations) – not really needed during training
- 2 x headtorches with spare batteries
- Survival bag/blanket
- First-aid kit
- Whistle and mobile phone
- Waterproof jacket – min 10,000mm hydrostatic head
- Long-sleeved fleece top – 150g minimum weight
- Long trousers/tights
- Spare T-shirt
- Cap
- Sunglasses
- Gloves
- Emergency food rations
- Map and route information
- Additional warm clothing in case of poor weather
- Cash for food en route
- Poles (optional)

LIST OF CICERONE'S INTERNATIONAL GUIDES

INTERNATIONAL CHALLENGES, COLLECTIONS AND ACTIVITIES

Canyoning in the Alps
Europe's High Points

ALPS CROSS-BORDER ROUTES

100 Hut Walks in the Alps
Alpine Ski Mountaineering
    Vol 1 – Western Alps
    Vol 2 – Central and Eastern Alps
Chamonix to Zermatt
The Karnischer Hohenweg
The Tour of the Bernina
Tour of Monte Rosa
Tour of the Matterhorn
Trail Running – Chamonix and the Mont Blanc region
Trekking in the Alps
Trekking in the Silvretta and Ratikon Alps
Trekking Munich to Venice
Trekking the Tour of Mont Blanc
Walking in the Alps

AFRICA

Walking in the Drakensberg
KilimanjaroThe High Atlas
Walks and Scrambles in the Moroccan Anti-Atlas

PYRENEES AND FRANCE/SPAIN CROSS-BORDER ROUTES

Shorter Treks in the Pyrenees
The GR10 Trail
The GR11 Trail
The Pyrenean Haute Route
The Pyrenees
Walks and Climbs in the Pyrenees

AUSTRIA

Innsbruck Mountain Adventures
The Adlerweg
Trekking in Austria's Hohe Tauern
Trekking in the Stubai Alps
Trekking in the Zillertal Alps

Walking in Austria
Walking in the Salzkammergut: the Austrian Lake District

EASTERN EUROPE

The Danube Cycleway Vol 2
The Elbe Cycle Route
The High Tatras
The Mountains of Romania
Walking in Bulgaria's National Parks
Walking in Hungary

FRANCE, BELGIUM AND LUXEMBOURG

Chamonix Mountain Adventures
Cycle Touring in France
Cycling London to Paris
Cycling the Canal de la Garonne
Cycling the Canal du Midi
Mont Blanc Walks
Mountain Adventures in the Maurienne
Short Treks on Corsica
The GR20 Corsica
The GR5 Trail
The GR5 Trail – Benelux and Lorraine
The GR5 Trail – Vosges and Jura
The Grand Traverse of the Massif Central
The Loire Cycle Route
The Moselle Cycle Route
The River Rhone Cycle Route
The Way of St James – Le Puy to the Pyrenees
Tour of the Queyras
Trekking in the Vanoise
Trekking the Cathar Way
Trekking the Robert Louis Stevenson Trail
Vanoise Ski Touring
Via Ferratas of the French Alps
Walking in Provence – East
Walking in Provence – West
Walking in the Ardennes
Walking in the Auvergne
Walking in the Briançonnais
Walking in the Dordogne

Walking in the Haute Savoie: North
Walking in the Haute Savoie: South
Walking on Corsica

GERMANY

Hiking and Cycling in the Black Forest
The Danube Cycleway Vol 1
The Rhine Cycle Route
The Westweg
Walking in the Bavarian Alps

IRELAND

The Wild Atlantic Way and Western Ireland
Walking the Wicklow Way

ITALY

Alta Via 1 – Trekking in the Dolomites
Italy's Sibillini National Park
Shorter Walks in the Dolomites
Ski Touring and Snowshoeing in the Dolomites
The Way of St Francis
Trekking in the Apennines
Trekking in the Dolomites
Trekking the Giants' Trail: Alta Via 1 through the Italian Pennine Alps
Via Ferratas of the Italian Dolomites Vols 1&2
Walking and Trekking in the Gran Paradiso
Walking in Abruzzo
Walking in Italy's Cinque Terre
Walking in Italy's Stelvio National Park
Walking in Sicily
Walking in the Dolomites
Walking in Tuscany
Walking in Umbria
Walking Lake Como and Maggiore
Walking Lake Garda and Iseo
Walking on the Amalfi Coast
Walking the Via Francigena pilgrim route – Parts 2&3

Walks and Treks in the
Maritime Alps

MEDITERRANEAN
The High Mountains of Crete
Trekking in Greece
Treks and Climbs in Wadi Rum,
Jordan
Walking and Trekking in Zagori
Walking and Trekking on Corfu
Walking in Cyprus
Walking on Malta
Walking on the Greek Islands –
the Cyclades

NEW ZEALAND
AND AUSTRALIA
Hiking the Overland Track

NORTH AMERICA
The John Muir Trail
The Pacific Crest Trail

SOUTH AMERICA
Aconcagua and the Southern
Andes
Hiking and Biking Peru's Inca
Trails
Torres del Paine

SCANDINAVIA, ICELAND
AND GREENLAND
Hiking in Norway – South
Trekking in Greenland – The
Arctic Circle Trail
Trekking the Kungsleden
Walking and Trekking in Iceland

SLOVENIA, CROATIA,
MONTENEGRO AND
ALBANIA
Mountain Biking in Slovenia
The Islands of Croatia
The Julian Alps of Slovenia
The Mountains of Montenegro
The Peaks of the Balkans Trail
The Slovene Mountain Trail
Walking in Slovenia: The
Karavanke
Walks and Treks in Croatia

SPAIN AND PORTUGAL
Camino de Santiago:
Camino Frances
Coastal Walks in Andalucia

Cycling the Camino de Santiago
Cycling the Ruta Via de la Plata
Mountain Walking in Mallorca
Mountain Walking in
Southern Catalunya
Portugal's Rota Vicentina
Spain's Sendero Historico: The
GR1
The Andalucian Coast to Coast
Walk
The Camino del Norte and
Camino Primitivo
The Camino Ingles and Ruta
do Mar
The Camino Portugues
The Mountains of Nerja
The Mountains of Ronda
and Grazalema
The Sierras of Extremadura
Trekking in Mallorca
Trekking in the Canary Islands
Trekking the GR7 in Andalucia
Walking and Trekking in the
Sierra Nevada
Walking in Andalucia
Walking in Menorca
Walking in Portugal
Walking in the Algarve
Walking on the Azores
Walking in the Cordillera
Cantabrica
Walking on Gran Canaria
Walking on La Gomera and El
Hierro
Walking on La Palma
Walking on Lanzarote
and Fuerteventura
Walking on Madeira
Walking on Tenerife
Walking on the Costa Blanca
Walking the Camino dos Faros

SWITZERLAND
Switzerland's Jura Crest Trail
The Swiss Alpine Pass Route –
Via Alpina Route 1
The Swiss Alps
Tour of the Jungfrau Region
Walking in the Bernese Oberland
Walking in the Engadine –
Switzerland
Walking in the Valais
Walking in Zermatt and Saas-Fee

JAPAN AND ASIA
Hiking and Trekking in the Japan
Alps and Mount Fuji
Japan's Kumano Kodo Pilgrimage
Trekking in Tajikistan

HIMALAYA
Annapurna
Everest: A Trekker's Guide
Trekking in the Himalaya
Trekking in Bhutan
Trekking in Ladakh

MOUNTAIN LITERATURE
8000 metres
A Walk in the Clouds
Abode of the Gods
Fifty Years of Adventure
The Pennine Way – the Path,
the People, the Journey
Unjustifiable Risk?

TECHNIQUES
Fastpacking
Geocaching in the UK
Map and Compass
Outdoor Photography
Polar Exploration
The Mountain Hut Book

MINI GUIDES
Alpine Flowers
Navigation
Pocket First Aid and
Wilderness Medicine
Snow

For full information on all our
guides, books and eBooks,
visit our website:
www.cicerone.co.uk

CICERONE

Trust Cicerone to guide your next adventure, wherever it may be around the world...

Discover guides for hiking, mountain walking, backpacking, trekking, trail running, cycling and mountain biking, ski touring, climbing and scrambling in Britain, Europe and worldwide.

Connect with Cicerone online and find inspiration.

- buy books and ebooks
- articles, advice and trip reports
- podcasts and live events
- GPX files and updates
- regular newsletter

cicerone.co.uk